STEP-BY-STEP
rugmaking

A Complete Introduction to the Craft of Rugmaking

By Nell Znamierowski

Conceived and edited by
William and Shirley Sayles

 **GOLDEN PRESS· NEW YORK**

WESTERN PUBLISHING COMPANY, INC.
Racine, Wisconsin

To my father and mother

Embroidered rug by Helen Znamierowski used as a table cover in the 1920's.

Library of Congress Catalog Card Number: 70–177273

Contents

ACKNOWLEDGEMENTS

In the course of preparing this book many craftsmen were asked for photographic examples of their work, and their cooperation was very gratifying—thanks go to them and to the American Craftsmen's Council. Thanks also to Regal Rugs, Inc., for photographs and permission to photograph rugs designed by Miss Znamierowski, and to Lee Nordness Gallery for those also made by Miss Znamierowski; and to Dorothy Liebes Design, Inc., for permission to use three examples of her work (one of which appears on the cover, bottom right).

Among those who have assisted in the preparation of this book, special thanks are due to:
Remo Cosentino, *Design and Production*
Stephen Manville, *Photography*
Dag Olsen, *Diagrams*

Introduction

A rug adorns the floor it is on and adds warmth and beauty to its surroundings. It can animate a room by providing striking patterns in bold colors, or it can be a quieting influence on a room filled with colors and patterns. It can be the focal point around which the room is gathered, or the divider that separates one part of the room from the other. But no matter how it functions, or how small in size or simple in design and technique it is, making it will be an exciting endeavor. You can work on the rug at odd moments throughout the day, when you "just feel like relaxing," or when you feel inspired. The basic processes of making the stitches, knots, or loops are few and, with application, are quickly learned and easily done following the information given in this book.

THE RUGMAKING TECHNIQUES

The rug techniques covered in this book are embroidery, latch hook, crochet, knitting, braiding, hooking, and weaving. The beginner will find that most of these techniques are quite simple, and that they lend themselves to further invention or exploration either alone or in conjunction with another technique.

Each of the techniques offered uses only a minimum of space: four—embroidery, latch hook, crochet, and knitting—are pick-up or lap work; braiding is easily accomplished on a table; most hooking requires a frame, and weaving a frame loom, but in both of these instances the equipment is easily stored away even while the rug is in progress.

TOOLS AND MATERIALS

The tools used are nominal in price and are life-lasting; some of them, such as the frame and frame loom, can be made at home. The materials are easy to come by no matter where you live; they are as near as your shopping area, mailbox, or ragbag. Basically, they fall into two categories—yarn and fabric. Other materials such as fur, leather, twine, and jute can also be experimented with and used.

The cost of the rug is as flexible as is the choice of materials. It can range from very high (where nothing is spared to get the exact colors and textures for a certain design effect) to very little (where worn or discarded clothing is used or where colors are home-dyed). Used materials are what rag rugs are all about—some of the most appealing rugs have been made from such materials. Most of the techniques, particularly hooking and braiding, lend themselves easily to used materials.

PLANNING THE RUG

Although technique and material are important considerations, it is on the subject of design that I hope this book will give the most confidence, instruction, and inspiration. Technique cannot be overlooked, but when the rug is finished, it will be the design, color,

One of twelve panels of an embroidered carpet by H.M. Queen Mary of England. Completed in 1950. Courtesy of The National Gallery of Canada, Ottawa.

The soft texture and color of a rug add warmth and beauty to a setting.
Hooked rug in wool yarn by Gloria Crouse.

(Above) Pictorial patterns knotted into rug with wool yarn. Finland, 1782. Courtesy of The National Museum, Helsinki.

(Left) Navajo blanket rug with geometric design. New Mexico. Courtesy of The Museum of the American Indian. An example of an early use of rugs.

and texture that will decide whether or not it is a truly successful accomplishment.

If one thinks of the work of peasant cultures throughout the world, and even of our Colonial forebears, one realizes that it is not necessary to have had art or design training in order to make charming patterns that speak with feeling and heart. Rather it is that bit of oneself that the rugmaker puts into his work that gives the rug its unique value.

Perhaps the most important standard to apply in designing is to do what pleases *you* and *your* family, and not to be influenced by preconceived notions of what you think a rug should look like. The standard to measure by is not whether a flower has the correct number of petals or whether the proportion or scale of an object is true to life, but rather whether you are making a straightforward, simple design of something that pleases you. A design or color mistake is nothing to be ashamed of—it is something to learn from. Even if lines that should be straight turn out crooked, or if the flowers are more fanciful than real-looking, the personally designed rug will have more true beauty and vitality than one that has been faithfully copied.

Size imposes no limits in choosing a technique since the rug can be worked in individual sections which are then joined together. Unusual rug shapes can be manipulated in just about any technique. However, it would not be wise for a beginner to attempt an oddshaped rug; this is something better left for the future. Hooking is probably the freest and easiest medium with which to attempt different shapes, but they are also possible with other techniques and should certainly be tried.

SAMPLERS

Before settling down to make the rug, practice first by making a sampler. I cannot emphasize too much the lessons that will be learned. Not only will you get the feel of the technique, but you can experiment with materials and see what happens to color when it is translated into yarn and fabric. You can also experiment with the stitches, knots, or loops, and can estimate the amount of material that will be necessary for the completed rug. Use the different variations on the technique that are presented and any others that you want to try. Experiment to your heart's content, then put what you have learned into the finished rug.

ABOUT THE BOOK

This book is meant to start you on your way as surely and as simply as possible. Each section describes another phase in making the rug.

A garden landscape forms the design of this 18th-century Persian rug. Fragment. Courtesy of The Metropolitan Museum of Art, Theodore M. Davis Collection.

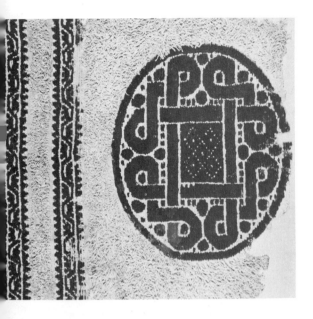

(Left) An early example of loop pile combined with cut pile. Loop pile in natural linen, cut pile in black wool. Egypt, 4th to 5th century. Courtesy of The Cooper-Hewitt Museum of Decorative Arts and Design, Smithsonian Institution. Gift of J. Pierpont Morgan.

(Below) Hooked bed rug from the Connecticut Valley, 1790. Note how rug is shaped to fit bed. An example of another use for rugs. Courtesy of The Brooklyn Museum. Randolph Levy Fund.

(Above) Strips of cloth worked into knitted base to form pile. Example is 6″ wide. Made by donor, Miss Maude M. Fierce. (Right) Detail of knitted pile rug. Courtesy of The Smithsonian Institution, Washington, D.C.

In some the emphasis is on yarn and fabric, color, texture, and design (some pointers on these are also included with the techniques). In others the emphasis is on practical considerations—that is, how to prepare for the work beforehand, how to dye colors, the different ways of finishing the rug, and how to care for it in the years to come—its cleaning, storage, and possible repair.

Projects. Each technique has its own section and within them are projects that you can do or design ideas that can be followed. These are intended to introduce you to the techniques and to the effects that are possible with them. But they are also meant as starting points for your own ideas. If you want to experiment by varying a project, by all means do so; these designs are such that you can adapt them to suit your own requirements.

The photographs that you will find throughout the book were chosen for their qualities of design and craftsmanship. They are here not only to show what can be accomplished but also to stimulate you toward developing your own designs.

With the knowledge that will be gained from the explanatory text and from the comprehensive diagrams and illustrations throughout, you should quickly gain confidence and be on your way to making your own rugs.

A FINAL TOUCH

Toward the finish of the rug, consider adding your name or initials and the date. It is a nice touch, and it adds to the pride you will have in your accomplishment. It is also an easy way of keeping a record of when the rug was made. You can, if you wish, incorporate these additions into the design on the front of the rug as was done in Colonial times. If you do so, work discreetly in a corner of the rug and in a color that is only a shade different from the one used in the background. Or you can embroider on the back of the rug, adding the title of the rug if it has one.

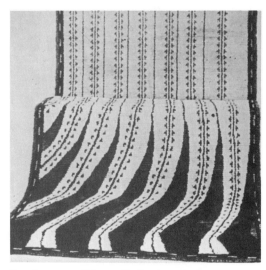

Bench rug, "Flame." Designed by Finnish artist Akseli Gallen-Kallela. Woven in 1913 by The Friends of the Finnish Handicraft, Helsinki.

REFERENCES

At the conclusion of this book is a list of suppliers for tools and materials, a list of books for further reading, and one of schools throughout the country that offer workshops in the various rug techniques.

GLOSSARY

Some of the most frequently used terms in this book are defined here for easy reference.

backing—any of various foundation materials through which some rugmaking techniques are worked.

cut pile—upright loops that are cut to form a velvety surface.

end—an individual length of yarn or other material; a warp thread or yarn.

filling—the widthwise material interwoven with the warp.

flat rug—a smoothfaced rug without pile.

flatweave—a woven rug without pile.

flossa—Scandinavian term for short knotted pile made over a pile gauge.

loop pile—upright loops that are left uncut.

pile—upright loops or cut ends that project from a foundation to form the wearing surface of a rug.

pile height—the height of pile measured from the surface of the backing to the top of the pile, not including the thickness of the backing.

ply—the number of single strands that have been twisted together in a length of yarn.

rya—pile in excess of 1″; average length is 2″–2½″. The name is Scandinavian in origin.

rya knot—the Ghiordes or Turkish knot used for rya pile. It can be formed in weaving, latch hook, or embroidery.

selvedge—side edges of a backing or woven rug so finished that they will not ravel. Neither binding nor hemming is required on tightly woven selvedges.

shag—a commercial name for rya.

warp—the threads or yarns running lengthwise in a fabric, between which the cross threads (filling) are woven.

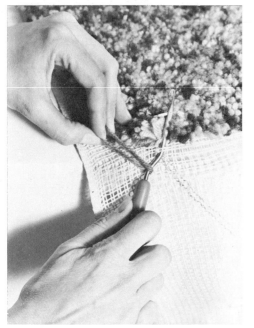

Making a rug by the latch-hook technique, with precut yarn on a mesh backing.

"Foliage," by Traute Ishida. 8′ × 6′. An example of imaginative use of the latch-hook technique. The shape and color scheme were dictated by the source of inspiration.

Detail by Helen Znamierowski

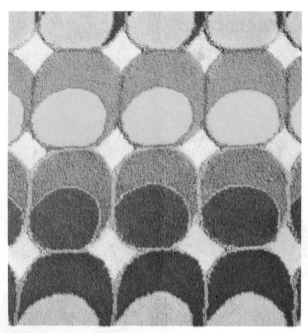

Detail, "Buds," by Traute Ishida

Embroidery

Just a few simple tools are all that are required in embroidery to create a rug of lasting pleasure and beauty. With needle, yarn, and a backing to embroider through (and sometimes a frame), you can work a wide and interesting variety of stitches.

The embroidery technique can be used to form rugs of quiet simplicity or of rich and varied textures. The stitches are not difficult to learn or do, and it is exciting to discover the many effects that can be obtained with knowledge of just a few simple ones. Such stitches can also be combined to achieve seemingly intricate designs. Almost any yarn or fabric, or mixture of yarns or fabrics, that can be threaded through a needle can be used. Embroidery is also an effective way to make a rya, or shag, rug.

This technique is also known as needlework, needlepoint, and tapestry work—the last because some of the stitches used in embroidery closely resemble those in woven tapestry rugs.

For this technique see pages 58–65.

Latch Hook

This technique is probably foolproof for the beginner; it is a simple and enjoyable way to make a strong, well-wearing rug of rich, deep-piled beauty. Since the technique is uncomplicated, you will find that you have freedom to concentrate on innovations.

You can learn how to use the latch hook in no time at all. The hook has a hinged latch attached that opens and closes to hold and then release the yarn. When the hook pulls the yarn through the backing foundation, it automatically forms it into a knot. The yarn is cut before it is used; this not only determines the length of the pile, but it also allows for the use of different yarns within the same area. In this way a lovely textural quality can be had, as well as a varicolored one.

Two repeat patterns are offered as projects in the latch-hook section. They can also be adapted for use in other techniques.

For this technique see page 66–69.

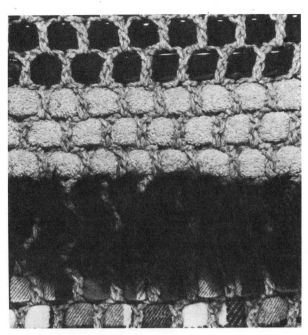

Detail of crochet filet mesh rug

Detail by Dorothy Liebes Design, Inc.

Crochet

The crochet technique produces a firm and solid structure that is particularly well suited to a rug. Only a few basic stitches form the foundation of this craft, but with them, other stitches can be developed.

Crochet goes quickly, and the rug is soon done. When thick yarn or wide rag strips are used in combination with a large-sized hook, the work goes even more quickly. In one of the crochet projects offered, additional texture is obtained in the crochet body by putting on either embroidery stitches or the rya knot at various intervals.

The rug detail shown above is an example of what can be accomplished with this fascinating craft. Strips of fabric, terry cloth, vinyl, and fur have been inserted in an interweaving manner throughout the width of a crocheted mesh base. Other materials—from rags and jute to stockings and felt—can also be used. The use of such materials not only makes for a visually exciting rug but for an economical one as well.

For this technique see pages 70–75.

Knitting

Like crochet, knitting is a method of constructing a rug out of yarn or fabric without depending on a backing foundation through which stitches must be worked. In company with the other rugmaking techniques given, knitted rugs can be made in individually worked sections which are later joined together to form the design. In this way you can made a large rug using weighty wools and still not have a heavy mass of material in your lap or an unwieldy amount of stitches on the knitting needles.

The fundamental stitches are not difficult to learn, and once you master them and become adept in the use of the needles, you will find that there is literally no end to the patterns that can be created.

Simple stitches are presented here that will form geometric patterns when they are knitted and joined together. Because of the closeness of the design possibilities in both knitting and crochet, the two techniques are presented together in one section.

For this technique see pages 70–75.

Detail by Gloria W. Scannell

Detail, "Aquatic Memories," by Ina Golub

Braiding

Braiding is a true hand craft: the fingers are the main tools, and all other equipment is incidental. As in crochet and knitting, no backing foundation is required. The structure of the braid determines the design, which can be primarily a simple one concerned with color and texture placement.

The technique of manipulating the braids is soon mastered; time can then be given to refinements on this technique. These will not only add to the enjoyment of braiding, but can contribute much to variety in color and design.

Long associated with thrift, braiding is also a fast, rhythmic method of producing a sturdy, long-lasting, and hard-wearing rug, pleasantly soft underfoot. The materials used are usually contents of the rag-bag and outgrown clothing, or fabrics obtained from remnant counters, thrift shops, or rummage sales. New fabrics, of course, can also be used, as can materials such as yarn, cord, or grasses.

For this technique see pages 76-79

Hooking

This is one of the most popular of all the rug-making techniques, and it shares with braiding a reputation for economy. Very often material left over from other techniques can be used to hook with.

The main tool (which can be a hand hook, punch needle, or speed hook) pulls or pushes the material through a backing to form loops on the right side. The loops can be left as they are, or can be sheared to form cut pile. You can work at your own speed in comfortable intimacy with a hand hook, or you can finish the rug more quickly by using a hook designed for fast work. Most hooking requires a frame to hold the backing taut.

Hooking is a technique that offers one of the greatest areas for design and creativity. The hook can draw pictorial designs or make any sort of line—from graceful and charming curves to zigzags or diagonals all going in several directions. Random textural effects are achieved by combining yarn and fabric, or by mixing cut and looped pile, or by cutting the pile to different levels.

For this technique see pages 80-85.

Detail by Solange Kowert

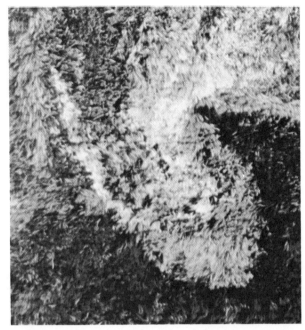

Detail, "Yin-Yang," by Nell Znamierowski

Weaving

In weaving, some sort of loom is required on which yarn can be stretched lengthwise to form what is known as the warp. Once that is done, yarns (or other materials) are passed over and under the warp widthwise to form the filling of the rug. This is not a complicated process, nor is it one in which the necessary skills take long to perfect.

The frame loom suggested on page 87 is a very simple one that can be constructed out of an old picture frame, a canvas stretcher, or four strips of wood. Just nails are required on which to stretch the warp yarns. The loom can be made small enough to hold in the lap, or of a larger size that will stand against the wall.

With either size, a flatweave or a pile rug can be made. Just about any material can be used (rag rugs are quickly completed), and the design potential is almost limitless.

For this technique see pages 86–93.

Pile Rugs

A pile rug consists of cut or uncut loops that project above its foundation to form the wearing surface. Short pile is ¼″ to 1″ high and is closely spaced so that it stands upright. The loops can be left intact or they can be cut to form a velvety-soft surface. In weaving, short pile is often referred to by its Scandinavian name, *flossa.*

Long pile is between 1″ and 4″, but the most commonly used heights are 2″ to 3″. Long loops are cut (so that heels will not catch in them), and are widely spaced so that the yarn falls every which way and subtly mutes definite designs and color outlines. This effect has been called shag, but it is perhaps better known by its Scandinavian name, *rya.*

Rya has also come to mean the knot employed in making embroidered, woven, or latch-hooked pile rugs. This knot is formed like the Ghiordes knot used in Oriental rugs. The hooking technique forms its own pile, and crocheted, knitted, or braided rugs can have the rya knot added, with the background usually left exposed in various areas as part of the pattern.

Yarns

There is a category of yarns designated as rug yarns that can be used for most of the techniques in this book. As a rule they are not identified by count (numerical designation of size or thickness), so unless you have the yarn in hand it will be difficult to know how thick it is. If you are purchasing by mail, request samples before placing your order.

Rug yarn is usually composed of two to six threads twisted together to form a single thread, or ply; from this come the designations of 2 ply, 3 ply, 4 ply, etc. On page 19 is a chart of rug yarn types. Those that I classify there as medium weight are mostly wool, although more and more synthetic yarns and blends are appearing. The medium weights have a somewhat stiff, inelastic surface as opposed to a knitting worsted, for example, which is very resilient and very soft. This hard surface, however, makes for excellent durability underfoot. Some of these yarns have been given pronounced twists to emulate the Scandinavian rya rug yarns. The lightweight yarns are finer, and the heavyweight ones thicker, usually ¼″ in diameter, and can be of wool but are more commonly of cotton, or of rayon and other synthetics. They have bulk built into them, and some types are surprisingly light in proportion to their thickness.

Knitting worsted and related yarns can also be used in rugs, but in limited quantities only and in combination with rug yarn. Because they are soft and without too much body, they will mat down and

The use of a variety of contrasting yarns. Detail of woven rug by Yvonne Palmer Bobrowicz.

The use of fabric strips. Detail of braided rug in wool by Gloria W. Scannell.

will not wear well when used alone. A beginner could start by using a variety of rug yarns and then add finer or more luxurious yarns as highlights or accents.

Fabrics

As with yarns, the tendency in fabrics has been to use primarily wool since it is resilient underfoot, wears well, and resists soiling. However, any cloth should be considered. Generally, medium-weight fabrics work best, such as those used in sportswear and trousers. Don't feel you have to concentrate on just solid colors; the use of prints, tweeds, plaids, or other patterns can add character and diversification to the rug. Patterns and solid colors, as well as various weights and textures, can be mixed together.

SOURCES FOR MATERIALS
Besides obtaining materials from local yarn and fabric stores, it would be wise to investigate what mail-order suppliers have to offer. They will send samples and price lists on request for a minimal charge. This is money worth spending, for not only will the samples help you decide what materials to use for the rug you are planning, but they are also a quick way of becoming acquainted with what is available so that you can get ideas, juggle costs, and begin plans for other rugs. A list of suppliers is at the end of this book; an additional list can be prepared by consulting needlecraft magazines.

By and large the most active senders of samples are the yarn producers and distributors. Most carry a variety of yarns in a virtual rainbow of colors. Dealing with many yarn sources should encourage you to mix yarn weights and types as well as colors. I happen to be partial to outlets for commercial rug yarns; these yarns are rug mill leftovers from the previous season's color line and are inexpensive. Some of these outlets do not send samples, but if you are fortunate enough to be in an area where there is an outlet, you can spend some pleasant and fruitful hours browsing among its bins.

Remnant counters and mill end stores are other excellent sources. In addition, do not overlook new uses for old or worn materials. Besides keeping the cost of the rug down, they will contribute a soft, mellow quality to the colors and add variation to the texture. Wool or synthetic yarns unraveled from discarded knitted or crocheted items can provide fresh materials, as can worn neckties, stockings or panty hose (in different colors and textures), torn sheets, blankets, bedspreads, bathrobes, coats, shirts, trousers, and faded blue denims. Your closets, or those of friends, will probably yield worn clothing ready to be discarded. Thrift shops and rummage sales are two other sources for perfectly good materials that, once taken apart, washed, and dyed (if desired), can be used to advantage. If you sew at home, you can use the scraps left over from fabric cuttings—they are ideal for dyeing and using in braiding or hooking.

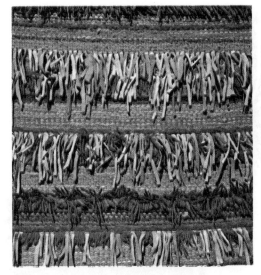

Two details of the imaginative use of materials. (Above) Leather strips and wool yarn. By Michelle Lester. (Below) Dyed sheepskin strips and yarn. By Pat Swenson.

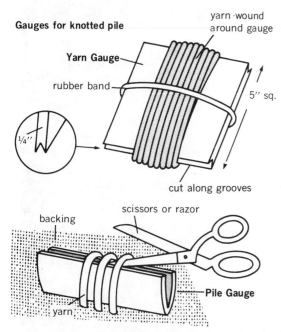

Examples of yarn samples available from producers or distributors.

Gauges for knotted pile

Yarn Gauge

rubber band

yarn wound around gauge

5" sq.

¼"

cut along grooves

backing

scissors or razor

Pile Gauge

yarn

Yarn gauge (top) for precutting yarn. Pile gauge (bottom) for continuous strand. To cut, use razor or scissors.

Preparing the Material

Washing fabrics. Before fabrics are cut for use they should be washed. (If you are using worn fabrics, prepare for washing by opening all seams or hems so that the cloth lies flat. Also remove any fasteners or facings, and cut out moth-eaten or worn areas.) Wash in hot water with a mild soap—use stronger soap if the fabric is soiled. Rinse and dry thoroughly. The hot water will shrink many of the woolens, as well as those materials that were not previously pre-shrunk, making it less likely that they will fray or pull apart. To test for colorfastness, wash a swatch of the fabric in hot water while rubbing with a strong soap.

Washing yarn. New yarn is usually clean and does not have to be washed, but yarn from a commercial rug yarn outlet should be washed to make it softer, and to rid it of any factory dirt. Yarn should be in skeins for washing. Tie a contrasting color cord around each skein in two or three places to hold it together loosely. Wash in lukewarm water and a small amount of soap flakes. Hang by the cord until thoroughly dry. Unraveled yarn should also be washed to remove the soil and kinks of previous use. Wash in the same manner; then, while still damp, wind into a ball or over a thin board to keep it taut and straight as it dries.

Yarn: skeins, balls, or cones. The washed and dried yarn can be left in skeins if it is to be precut for any of the rya techniques, or if it is to be wound onto shuttles for weaving. For other techniques, wind into balls so that it will feed off easily. The balls can be put into boxes while in use to prevent them from rolling over the floor. Yarn that did not have to be washed can be wound off directly from whatever form it comes in—skein, ball, or cone—but should be in a ball or on a cone for any technique where it must feed off smoothly.

CUTTING YARN FOR KNOTTED PILE

Yarn for the rya (Ghiordes) knot can be precut around a yarn gauge or looped in a continuous strand around a pile gauge. With pile gauge, the work goes quickly; with yarn gauge, color and texture can be changed with every knot. Both methods are described below.

Pile gauge—for use with continuous strand of yarn (see diagram). Metal pile gauges are available at weaving supply houses, but, because of their weight and long lengths, are used only in weaving. However, a pile gauge made at home out of wood or cardboard can be used in weaving and embroidery. Its height will be determined by the intended depth of the pile, which usually ranges from ¼" to 2", and its length by your needs—usual lengths are 9" to 12". Gauges of different heights can be used in one rug or even in one row. If you are making a wooden gauge, carve a v-shaped groove in it so that a single-edge razor blade can glide through to cut the loops. If you are making a cardboard gauge, use two extra-heavy pieces of cardboard and tape them together at sides and bottom. Leave the top free so that the yarn can be cut by blade or scissors. In place of a gauge, use a ruler or knitting needle for low pile, and your hand or fingers for uneven pile.

To use the gauge, place it flat on the rug foundation. In the embroidery technique, the needle bearing the yarn is brought around the gauge to help form the knot (bottom page 61). In weaving, a yarn bundle called a butterfly is used. Slide the gauge across the rows as each section is completed. If you want looped pile, leave the yarn as is, but if you want cut pile, slash loops with a razor before moving gauge.

Yarn gauge—for precutting yarn (see diagram). Although you can buy yarn already cut, cutting your own takes very little time and will enable you to use a variety of yarns. It is also more economical since you can take advantage of yarn sales or use up any leftovers on hand. An automatic yarn cutter for this purpose cuts the yarn into uniform 2½″ lengths. This length will make a pile of ¾″ to 1″ (the rest of the yarn is taken up in the knotting process), which is the height usually used for latch-hooked rugs. For more leeway in the choice of pile heights, you can make your own gauge out of wood or heavy cardboard.

A wooden gauge is more durable than a cardboard one and can be made from one piece of ¼″ thick scrap wood. This thickness will allow you to cut grooves ⅛″ deep into the widthwise edges so that a mat knife or single-edge razor blade can glide smoothly through to cut the yarn. Cut the wood to twice the length of the desired pile height, plus 1″ takeup for the knot. It need not be more than 4″ to 5″ wide, and should be smoothly sanded so there will be no rough edges for the yarn to catch on. A cardboard gauge uses two pieces, but is cut to the same dimensions. Tape the lengthwise edges together, leaving the widthwise ones free to act as tracks for the cutting tool.

Wind the yarn as shown. This does not have to be done meticulously; just wind quickly, piling strand upon strand until a substantial amount is on gauge, up to ¼″ thick at the edges. Put a rubber band around the yarn so it will not fall away when cut. Then slit through both grooves. (The lengths will not all be precisely the same, which I find is the best way to get a rya with a shaggy texture.) The cut lengths can be stored in plastic bags or in boxes.

CUTTING FABRICS

Before fabric can be used in any of the techniques, it has to be cut or torn into strips. The widths of the strips will vary according to the technique used. If wide widths are needed, cut or tear the fabric lengthwise on the straight or on the bias, depending on the material. For example, cut or tear woven fabrics on the bias so that they will not fray, and knitted ones on the straight. Stockings are cut into strips. For narrow widths, use sharp, long-bladed shears or a fabric cutter (page 20). Using the torn straight edge of the

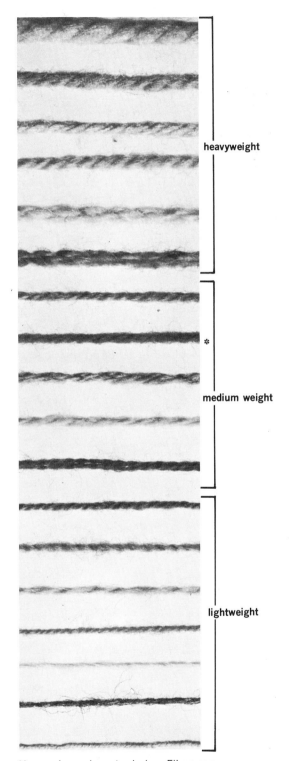

heavyweight

*

medium weight

lightweight

Yarns shown in actual size. Fiber contents are wool, cotton, and assorted synthetics. All are rug yarns except *knitting worsted.

(Above) Prepared fabric. Note wound, flat rolls of continuous lengths, and very narrow strips cut for hooking.

(Below) Fabric strip cutter. Model shown has interchangeable blades that cut 3/32" to 2" widths.

Bias joining for continuous strips

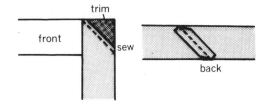

fabric as a guide, measure out and cut to the widths needed. Tight weaves and jerseys can be cut into fairly thin strips for hooking. Precut jersey strips, available by the skein or bagful, are wider and can be used in a variety of techniques.

The fabric cutter is an extremely convenient tool and worthwhile investing in if you plan to work quite a bit with fabrics. There are slight variations in the models available, but most have interchangeable blades for different widths. When blades become dulled they can be returned to the factory for regrinding at a nominal cost.

When you begin the rug, cut just enough fabric for a couple of day's work in case you change your mind and decide to use a different fabric. Place cut fabric in plastic bags or open boxes so you can see what is on hand. Knowing what fabrics you have can inspire design ideas, and will help you decide on accompanying materials. To join fabric in continuous strips for certain techniques, see diagram, below.

PRACTICAL CONSIDERATIONS
You will, of course, want the rug you have made to wear well and to have a reasonable life span. In most cases wearability will be a matter of traffic patterns. If you put the rug where there is much traffic, it will wear out more quickly than it will where traffic is less. The selection of durable materials, and the way less durable ones are used, will also assure a longer life for the rug. Wool of inferior quality, and certain types of linen, can be combined with a stronger material for better durability. This is also a solution for somewhat fragile materials.

For the longest wear, the best solution is to use synthetics, or wool with a hard twist and a long staple (length of fiber). The construction and density of the rug are also deciding factors. A rug with a high pile, for example, will wear longer than a flat rug, or one with a very short pile.

Another consideration is the adaptability of the material to the technique used. A certain amount of experimentation is healthy, but if you find you are forcing the tools of the technique to accommodate the material, then that material is not for that technique. Either choose a different technique or settle for another material.

ESTIMATING COST AND AMOUNTS
A question many readers may have is how much a first rug will cost, and how to estimate that cost. The answer is not easy, for it all depends on the technique used and on the source and type of material. Obviously a rug for which all the material has been bought brand new will cost more than a rug in which some, or all, of the material is being reused or is left over from another project. Also, a rug made of different types of material in various colors will cost more than one in only two or three colors, or even one for which you have dyed the colors yourself. This is because

yarns and fabrics cannot always be obtained in small amounts, and you may end up with a lot of leftovers. However, the use of those leftovers can serve to defray the cost of your next rug. So cost becomes relative, and, although every rugmaker would like to keep expenses down, this consideration should not overshadow the pleasure obtained in making the rug. Also, you will have a one-of-a-kind item that, even if you could buy it in a store, would cost many times what you spent for the material.

Making a sampler. The best way to estimate cost when using new materials is to make a small sampler 3″ or 4″ square. If you want, it can be up to 1′ square, but no larger than that. Use material you have at home that approximates the weight you plan to buy, or else buy as small an amount as possible. The sampler will also serve to introduce you to the technique, as well as help you decide on color, density, texture, and pattern. In terms of lessons learned, a sampler is worth its weight in gold. If, after making it, you find yourself still undecided about some aspect of the rug, then I suggest you make a small rug (about 2′ × 3′) before you tackle a large one.

Based on the weight of the sampler, you can estimate the cost of the rug. For example, if a 1′ sampler uses x amount of yarn, multiply x amount by the number of square feet in the planned rug to arrive at the total weight. (To calculate square feet, see chart below.) Once you know the weight of the rug, multiply weight by the price of the material to calculate the cost of the rug. When techniques, pile heights, and materials are to be mixed, the cost would then be a common sense averaging of the three factors.

If you have made a sketch of your planned rug and have designated the color areas, you will be able to estimate the apportioning of each color. For example, color A may appear to be in ¼ of the rug, color B in another ¼, and color C in ½. By dividing these amounts into the total weight, you will know how many pounds of each color to buy.

A sampler helps determine cost, yarn amounts, and design, and gives experience in the technique. The sampler shown eventually resulted in a 4′ × 7′ rug. By Ferne Jacobs.

How to calculate square footage.

4′ × 6′ = 24 square ft.

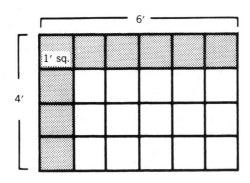

Calculate square feet by multiplying outside dimensions. The example shown represents a 4′ × 6′ rug. It equals 24 sq. ft., or 24 1′ squares.

Backings

The backing forms the foundation of the rug in embroidery, hooking, and latch hook, and is the cloth through which these techniques are worked. Since the backing will be holding the stitches, knots, or loops together, it is important to buy one that is durable. However, durability is usually a matter of many years even with backings that are regarded as less durable than others. Basically, wear depends on traffic patterns, the surface the backing is lying on (carpeting or type of floor), and whether the rug is lined for added protection.

As for expense, burlap is the most reasonable, but if you want to be even thriftier you can use feed and grain sacks. Choose those that are sturdy, open their seams, and use only for small rugs unless you do not mind joining sacks together for larger ones. Many lovely hooked and embroidered rugs of the past century were made on such humble backings. A worn rug can also be reincarnated as the backing for a new hooked or embroidered one.

When buying backing, choose one suitable for the technique and in the width necessary for the rug. Be sure to allow for the hem and a little more for possible measuring error. If you plan to work selvedge to selvedge, leave at least ½″ on each side for a narrow hem. Shown facing page, top, is a list of common backings that can be bought by the yard, together with their maximum widths. The average popular width seems to be 40″, which would be sufficient for a 3′ rug with a 2″ hem all around. If you have leftover widths that you wish to use, they can be sewn together either before, during, or after working the rug. (See Joining, page 30.)

It would be best for a beginner to hook a first rug on burlap, since it is a porous fabric and therefore easy to hook through. For the first attempt at embroidery, a stiffer backing—rug warp cloth or canvas mesh—would be best. If you want to do just a long rya knot row by row, Scandinavian backing is the perfect choice, but if you want to mix techniques or have different pile heights, then you must use a backing that will allow you to place the rows wherever you wish and to use a variety of stitches. Canvas mesh is usually used for latch hook. Some backings have vertical and horizontal guidelines for stitch counting and for transferring designs.

Working size. To prepare backing, cut it to its working size (finished size plus 2″ hem all around), then draw outside shape of the rug on it. Overcast backing edges with strong thread to prevent fraying. Soft backings can be machine sewn. Or a doublefold bias binding can be put on and machine sewn. This makes a finished edge ready for hemming, and no overcasting is necessary. Canvas mesh edges can be covered with tape (plastic, adhesive, or masking). Remove tape when rug is completed. If you are planning a shape other than a rectangular one, do not cut shape out until the rug is finished and you are ready to make the hem.

Heavy upholstery or drapery fabrics can be used as backing with areas left exposed to form part of the design. Here a linen fabric is hooked through certain sections.

Maximum backing widths. Most of the backings listed are available in narrower widths.

Backing	Maximum width	Backing	Maximum width
Burlap	96″	Rug warp cloth	200″
Canvas mesh	79″	Jute	144″
Monk's cloth	184″	Scandinavian	39″

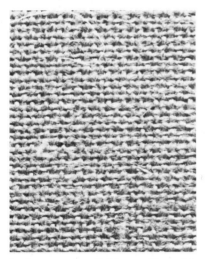

Burlap—most suitable quality is 12 to 14 oz. A finer weight would probably not wear as well. Used in embroidery and hooking.

Canvas mesh—a stiff mesh made up of doubled vertical and horizontal threads. Best for rug are 3½ or 4 holes per inch. Used in embroidery and latch hook.

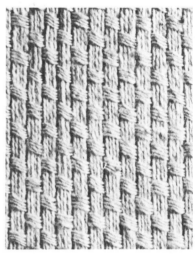

Monk's cloth—soft, durable cotton in a close weave. This pliable fabric comes in various qualities; almost all are suitable for embroidery or hooking.

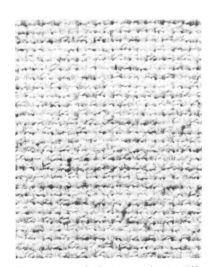

Rug warp cloth—somewhat stiff, quite heavy, and very strong. A high quality cotton, available in 2 or 3 weights. Used in embroidery and hooking.

Jute—a variety of weaves and weights, with guidelines for latch hook or embroidered rya knots. By shifting threads, embroidery or latch hook can be worked in any area.

Scandinavian—firmly woven of linen and wool with ⅝″ of backing between each row of spaces (unwoven warp). Embroidered rya knot is made in spaces.

Frames

The purpose of a frame is to stretch the backing and hold it taut. Usually used for soft backings in embroidery and hooking, it can also serve as a simple frame loom in weaving. (It is not necessary to stretch stiff backings in embroidery.) A frame is essential when hooking is done with a speed hook or an electric needle, less so than when done with a hand hook, although many hand hookers prefer to work on a taut backing. Those using a punch needle also work according to preference. A frame is also essential in weaving since the warp threads must be stretched to allow the filling to be woven through. A frame can be used as a loom in much the same fashion as Indian looms are in the American Southwest and in Central and South America.

The backing is usually attached to a frame with long thumb tacks, staples, or by lacing. When making a large rug on a small frame, fold the backing for convenience and attach through the folds. The backing on an oval frame is secured by tightening the top loop over the lower one.

There are lap frames and standing frames. The lap frame is small

---

TOOLS IN GENERAL

The following tools are used for all the techniques:

Scissors—bent-handled ones are particularly good for cutting loops and trimming pile (ordinary sharp scissors will also do the job, but these make it easier).

Tape measure, ruler, or yardstick—many uses, among them establishing the size and boundary of the rug.

Rug or tapestry needle—for overcasting hems and other sewing needs.

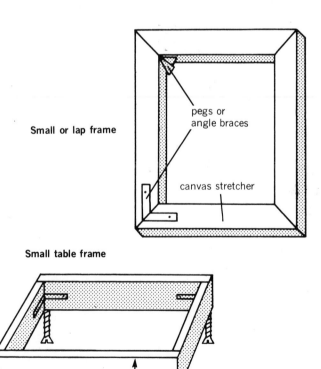

Small or lap frame

pegs or angle braces

canvas stretcher

Small table frame

3″ 5″

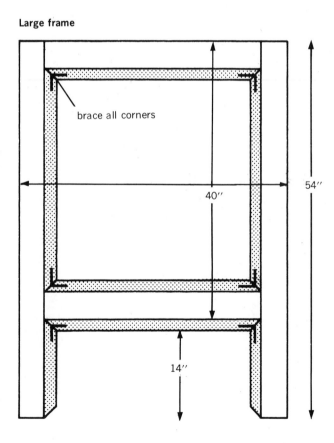

Large frame

brace all corners

40″ 54″

14″

enough to have one end sit comfortably in the lap while the other is propped against a table. It is an excellent learning tool, but is practical only for making small rugs or rug sections.

TO MAKE

Lap frame (facing page). Easily and inexpensively made out of canvas stretchers available in various sizes at art supply stores—or use a spare picture frame. The frame can also be constructed out of four strips of lumber, 1½″ wide × ½″ thick. The wood can be slightly wider, but not narrower. Either miter (cut at 45° angles) the strips at each end or square the corners. Nail corners and secure further with metal braces.

The frame should not be larger than 20″ × 26″ and preferably smaller. A larger size would be too heavy and awkward to manage. Also, the wood might buckle if its thickness is not equal to the weight of the work put upon it (only in embroidery would this not present a problem). For embroidery or hooking, leave enough clearance between the pattern area and the frame edges so your hand will not hit the frame while working the technique.

Table frame (facing page). A unique frame for speed hooking can be made by attaching four long bolts at each corner of a lap frame. They will act as legs, and will enable the frame to stand on a table. Bolts should be large, heavy, and flat-topped.

Large frame (facing page). To accommodate a rug about 4′ × 6′, use slats of wood at least 2″ × 4″ and attach as in the lap frame. This large frame can then be propped against a wall so that you can sit in front of it to work. For foot room, extend the lengthwise sides so that the working part of the frame is raised above the floor. (For a weaving frame, the bottom bar should be lower than shown to allow more working area; also, make vertical sides longer than horizontal ones.) The frame can also be supported across chair backs or sawhorses, or you can screw in the type of legs that are sold for cocktail tables. If the frame is quite large, it can be supported further by adding a leg to the middle of each length. You can then sit by the side of this frame while working, but eventually you will have to stand to reach the center.

TO BUY

Small frames on trestle stands have oval, round, or rectangular tops that tilt to any desired angle. As one area of the rug is finished, the work is removed from the frame and shifted to an unworked area. Refinements on these frames are found in the large rectangular ones that are primarily for hooking. Their tops also tilt, and most of the stands can be adjusted to comfortable working heights. Some of the tops are equipped with rollers so that as one area is finished it can be rolled out of the way to expose an unworked area. All frames fold for storage and can be moved easily from one area to another.

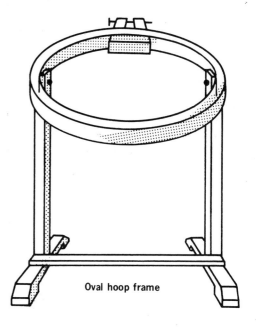

Oval hoop frame

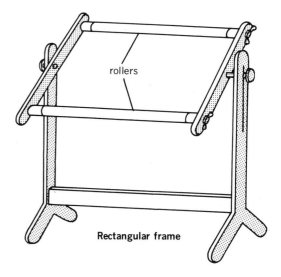

rollers

Rectangular frame

Transferring Designs

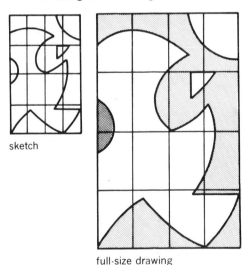

Large cutout shapes in paper for rug design. By Lynden Keith Johnson.

To enlarge sketch with grid

sketch

full-size drawing

To make a full-size drawing. Draw a grid over sketch and then, using the same number of grids, redraw design larger. Cross at correct spot from one grid to another.

Unless you are planning a free-form rug (one that is designed as it is being made), it is advisable to have a sketch of your rug to work from. The sketch will be a miniature of the rug and need not be elaborate; it is meant as a guide to color, yarn, and texture placement. Once the sketch is made, it is transferred to a form that will enable you to copy it as a rug. There are a number of ways of doing this; the most generally used ones are given here.

Points to remember: Allow for the rug hem when transferring the sketch. If backing is used, cut it to its working size (finished size plus hem allowance), then draw the outside shape of the rug. Use a soft pencil to trace lines, since you may have to erase several times. Go over the final lines with a felt-tipped pen.

SCALE DRAWING (GRAPH PAPER)

Draw the sketch on tracing paper, indicating where major changes in design, color, texture, or pile height occur, then turn it face down and go over pattern outlines on the back with a soft pencil. Turn face up again, tape to graph paper, and retrace lines, being sure to include the outside boundaries; the pencil marks on the back will transfer to the graph paper. Graph paper (available at stationery or art supply stores) is marked off into a number of squares per inch; the squares come in a variety of sizes. For the beginner, large sizes would be best—either 8 × 8 (8 sqs. to inch) or 10 × 10 (10 sqs. to inch).

Establish a scale so that a set amount on the graph-paper drawing equals a set amount on the rug; for example, 1″ on the drawing could equal ½′ on the rug, or 1′ or 2′. Once this is done you will know what each square equals in terms of the technique; that is, one square could equal one embroidery stitch; or, if you want to pinpoint inches in a hooking or weaving design, one square could equal ¼″.

Counting is an important part of this method. Squares and backing threads or stitches must be counted to assure that changes occur at the same time on graph and on rug. In some cases, especially in techniques using rya knots, you may want coded symbols or color markings to make counting knots easier and to denote where color changes occur.

The advantage to this method is that you do not have to transfer the pattern further or draw it to its full size. It also makes for a very compact working procedure. Use the original sketch for design and color reference.

FULL-SIZE DRAWING (GRIDWORK)

Although you will probably adopt the above method as you make more rugs, you may, as a beginner, prefer to make a full-size drawing from your sketch. To do so, draw a grid over the sketch, dividing it into halves and quarters as shown to the left. Then, on wrapping paper, draw outline of rug and corresponding grid. Transfer design as shown. A full-size drawing can also be done free-hand (without a grid) on the wrapping paper. The drawing can be used to double-check the progress of the rug in crochet, knitting, braiding, and weaving since the work areas in those techniques cannot be plotted as precisely as in techniques that use backing. In weaving, the full-size drawing can be pinned to the back of a frame or upright loom.

DIRECT TRANSFER

The full-size drawing is transferred directly to the backing by means of dress-maker's carbon (coated paper) or any good quality black carbon paper. Tape together as many carbons as needed and pin them to backing. Pin the wrapping paper over them and trace over your design with a tracing wheel (top right) or a blunt pencil. If the backing is canvas mesh you may not need carbon paper; just tape drawing *under* the backing. Since the mesh is so open, you can follow the lines of the design and mark them on the canvas with a felt-tipped pen. If you have difficulty seeing the drawing through the mesh, then make a carbon tracing.

REVERSE TRACING

When a rug is to be hooked with a punch needle or speed hook, a reverse tracing is made since hooking in this case is done on the back and is pushed through to the front. (Symmetrical designs don't have to be reversed.) With a dark wax crayon draw the lines of the design on the *face* side of the full-size drawing. Pin drawing face down on the backing and press with a hot iron. Or you could make a scale drawing, tape it face side against a window, and trace the lines as they appear through the back of the paper. Use this reverse side as the model for a full-size drawing. Then place this drawing over carbon paper and trace onto the backing.

The wax crayon method can be used instead of carbon paper when working on the front of the backing. First make a reverse tracing, then place it against a window, and trace over the lines. Go over them with the wax crayon and iron as before.

CUTOUTS

If the shapes are simple or repetitive, cut them out of cardboard and trace around them onto the backing, matching their placement to the original sketch.

HELPFUL HINTS

1. Work on the floor while making the full-scale drawing. Stand away every so often to get the proper perspective. Place yarn where various colors will fall in order to see the total effect. Or, instead of the floor, work at a table that you can tack to or tape on.

2. Colored pencils or crayons may be used in place of a felt-tipped pen. You might also want to color in whole areas, particularly with canvas mesh, where a single line does not show up too well. Remove excess crayon by pressing over a paper towel with a hot iron.

Direct transfer

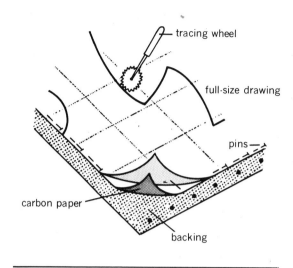

tracing wheel
full-size drawing
pins
carbon paper
backing

To make circle

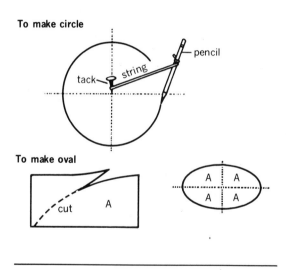

pencil
tack — string

To make oval

cut — A

A A
A A

Designing with cutouts

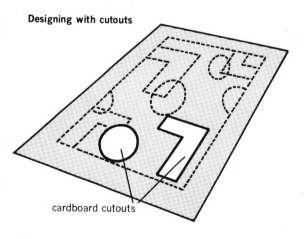

cardboard cutouts

Corners of pliable backings can be folded instead of mitered. Jute backing shown.

Finishing

To insure that a rug will keep its shape and remain attractive, some steps are taken at its finish. From the outset, thought should be given to how the rug will be finished—that is, how it will be hemmed or bound; whether it will have fringes or tassels; if in sections, how it will be joined; and whether to add a lining. Although a few can be last-minute decisions, in some techniques, provisions have to be made ahead of time.

Hemming and Binding

The backing for hooked, latch-hooked, and embroidered rugs must be either hemmed or bound to cover the raw edges and prevent them from raveling. Woven rugs and Scandinavian backings have two edges to hem or bind (the other two are selvedges). Braided, crocheted, and knitted rugs have self-finished edges produced by their techniques and are usually not bound, though binding can be put on to add strength and to help maintain a stable shape.

When making the hem at the completion of the rug, turn hem allowance to the back, folding it as close to the last row of stitches as possible, and pin in place. Do not fold so close or pull so tight that edge loops or knots separate and the backing shows through. A rug with high pile can be folded closer to the edge than one with low pile. Be careful in flat rugs, such as embroidered ones, not to have hem stitches show on the surface. Use carpet thread, heavy-duty cotton thread, or yarn in matching colors. A large-eyed tapestry needle or a curved rug needle can be used for stiff backings and woven rugs. Press hem flat.

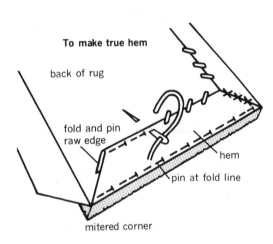

To make true hem

back of rug

fold and pin raw edge

hem

pin at fold line

mitered corner

Rug binding gives a strong, well-wearing edge and can be sewn on at the start of the rug or at its finish. It is available by the yard in 1¼″ to 1½″ widths and comes in neutral colors that you can dye to match the rug if you wish. Press-on bindings can also be used.

For soft, pliable backings that are not to be bound, make a true hem and miter or square the corners. Fold hem twice (see left). The second fold is minimal, just enough to hide the raw edges.

Canvas mesh. When folding hem allowance back, make sure its holes and threads match precisely with those on the back of the rug. If you want to make the hem before beginning the rug, pin in place and cross-stitch to the underside. Place stitches about ½″ from raw edges. Miter the corners (see A and B to left). When the rug is finished, sew binding as close to hem fold as you can and still have enough left over to cover the raw edges. Sew binding over edges (pull thread firmly but not too tightly). Miter corners by folding.

If you want to work selvedge to selvedge in order to get the most economy from the backing, leave a minimum of ½″ at each selvedge:

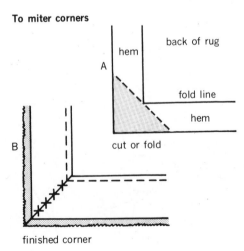

To miter corners

hem

A

back of rug

fold line

hem

B

cut or fold

finished corner

just enough to turn back and have binding attached. It is easier to work on the rug if the selvedge is hemmed when rug is finished.

Soft backing. The rug can be hemmed or have binding attached before work begins. Place binding on right side of backing, ½″ from pattern edge, and machine-stitch or hand-sew in place. When rug is completed, trim hem allowance to within ½″ of binding. Sew binding to back of rug. If binding is attached when rug is finished, sew it on close to rug edge and continue as before.

Round or oval rugs. To bind these shapes, obtain strong cotton fabric and cut on the bias into 2″ wide strips. Seam on the bias into a length to go around the rug. Pin close to pattern edge, right sides meeting, and sew together. When rug is completed, turn binding and hem margin to underside and sew, easing around the curves as you go. On canvas mesh you will have to equalize the excess fullness by first slitting the backing.

If binding is not used, make a true hem, but still equalize excess. On soft backings, ease hem gradually around the curves as you sew, then try to steam the excess so it will lie flat, or make many small pleats, taking care they do not become so bulky as to cause ripples or bumps on the surface. You can also slit the hem (top right).

Scandinavian backings and woven rugs. The finished rug can be bound as above, but only on its non-selvedge edges. Place binding farther away from hem foldline, as shown to right, or leave less hem allowance. Fold Scandinavian backing on one of its open rows. A woven rug has no such line to follow, so be sure the fold is straight. Before binding or hemming a woven rug you must make certain the filling will remain secure. To do so, knot the warp ends (see Finishing, page 93) or darn them into hem allowance (bottom left). Or overcast edges with blanket stitch (page 58). Use filling yarn.

If backing is not to be bound, overcast its edges neatly, turn allowance back, and sew down. If a woven rug is flexible enough, a true hem can be made. Both can also be finished with a Swedish braid.

Swedish braid. This very simple type of finishing makes a plaited, straight edge that can be left as is or can be turned back for the hem. Allow 4″ for the braid, in addition to the 2″ for the hem. In Scandinavian backing, unravel the 4″ in order to make the braid. In a woven rug, leave that amount unwoven.

To make the braid, turn rug face down, and, starting at the left, take in hand at least 4 single warp ends or 4 groups of ends (the number in each group depends on how close the warp ends are to each other). Interweave them under-over (see right), until only 4 ends are left at the far right. Make a short braid with these, whip its ends (see page 34), and trim. As you braid, push the strands toward the rug edge with your thumb. This will insure a tight edge. You will be left with a series of warp ends all pointing into the rug. With a needle, darn them into the rug edge as invisibly as possible. Trim ends flush. The braid can be left as is or sewn to back of rug. If you use an odd number of ends, start over-under.

To hem round or oval rug

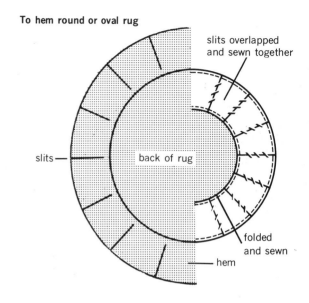

slits overlapped and sewn together

slits

back of rug

folded and sewn

hem

To bind non-selvedge edges

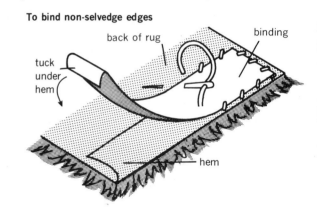

back of rug

binding

tuck under hem

hem

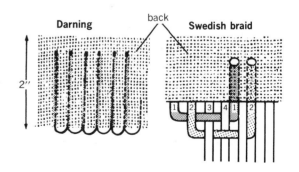

Darning — back — Swedish braid

2″

Darning individual warp ends into hem (left): Pull ends in tight for 2″. Trim.

Swedish braid (right): End #1 goes under 2, over 3, under 4. Surface and point toward rug.

Blocking and Pressing

Blocking—a wetting and stretching-out process, with a heated iron applied if necessary, to stabilize shape of the rug. Place layers of wrapping paper on a board, worktable, or floor. (Plastic sheeting or newspapers can be put down first to protect the work surface.) Outline on the wrapping paper the desired shape and size of the rug or rug sections. Dampen rug with cool to lukewarm water. Fasten it in position as shown to left and continue dampening to keep it pliable. If rug is still misshapen, repeat the process.

Steam pressing—a finishing touch for the rug, but usually not necessary. A steam iron can be used, but I find more steam is generated by wetting a large cloth with hot water, wringing it out before placing on the rug, and then pressing with a medium hot to hot iron. (Do not apply too much pressure or stitches may flatten.) I prefer to steam the rug rather than actually press it. In this case, hold a steam iron about ½″ above the wet cloth and move it very slowly over the surface without touching it.

Application. If the rug has been made in sections, it can be blocked or pressed after it has been joined, but it is much easier and often more desirable to do it while it is still in sections.

A rug pulled out of shape should be blocked, as should all knitted and crocheted rugs. A braided rug with ruffled edges, or a bump in its center due to uneven construction, *may* be helped by soaking both sides with warm water put on with a sponge. Try to flatten out bulges with your hands. If this doesn't work, then try steam pressing. Steaming usually improves the appearance of low pile rugs and those with certain yarns (usually synthetics) by causing the cut pile to bloom, or fill out. An embroidered or flatweave rug can be pressed face up or down. If for some reason the backing of a shag rug has buckled, press or steam *lightly* from the back.

Note: All damp rugs should be laid flat and face up to dry. Do not use a rug until it is completely dry. Keep in mind that these procedures take time, and will sometimes have to be repeated.

Joining

Joining, also known as piecing, is generally done for one of two reasons: the rug would be too heavy or too large to work as one piece, or the backing used is in narrow widths (because it is not available wider or because you wish to use up leftovers).

Blocking. Fasten dampened rug with rust-proof tacks or T pins. Start at one end and place about ½″ apart, squaring corners and keeping opposite side parallel. Do not remove until rug is completely dry. Sampler by Mary Walker Phillips.

When cutting a backing into sections, or when using narrow widths, remember to allow for hemming. Overcast all raw edges by hand or put in one row of fine machine stitches close to the edges.

A large-eyed tapestry needle or curved rug needle can be used for joining. Use carpet or heavy-duty cotton thread for embroidered, hooked, and latch-hooked rugs. Crocheted, knitted, and woven rugs can use the same yarn as in the rug. A rug lacer and lacing cord can be used for braided rugs.

Since one of the reasons for joining is that you wish to work in small areas, probably the only time you would join backing before work on the rug begins is when you are using narrow backing widths. Narrow widths, and sections, can also be joined while work is in progress or when it is finished.

Joining unworked backings. This type of joining is permanent, since it involves overlapping the backing and then working the technique through the doubled areas. For soft backings, overlap two backing pieces for 2″ so that the horizontal threads of both meet and match. Having them coincide perfectly will make it easier when hooking or stitching through the double seam. Pin in place and sew together along both edges of the overlap. For canvas mesh, overlap for 1″ to 1½″. Match holes and threads precisely, then overcast securely together. For burlap sacks, overlap selvedges by at least ⅜″ and non-selvedge edges by ¾″.

Joining while work is in progress. Join as before, but mark on the backings the point where you have to stop work in order to allow enough for the overlap (see diagram at bottom left of page 32). Pin and sew in place along both edges, using strong thread. Then proceed with the technique, stitching or hooking through the newly joined areas.

Joining completed sections. This method of joining applies to all techniques, including those not worked on backings. Finish off sections as you would a rug, then assemble them face down on the floor or table (joining is done from the back). If design is intricate, or there are many sections, draw the finished rug size on the floor with chalk, or with crayons on newspapers that have been taped together. Arrange sections to fit the pattern and make any necessary adjustments by adding or removing stitches, knots, or loops. If the sections are large, pin them together or tack with thread every few inches. This will prevent them from shifting while being joined.

The joining stitch is a simple lacing one that moves from one section to the other, drawing them together to meet. The length of the yarn or thread used should be about twice that of one side of a section.

An example of the creative joining of two widths that were woven separately. The seam was planned as part of the design. Yugoslavian rug, 6′2″ × 12′ 11″. Courtesy of The Textile Museum Collection, Washington, D.C. Gift of Mrs. Jelisaveta S. Allen.

Attach it securely to lower edge of the right section by looping it around edge threads a few times. Do not make knots. The first stitch will go through the left section. (See diagram below to make stitch.) At completion of seam, loop yarn around top threads two or three times to secure. Run back under last stitches and clip off. Space stitches about ¼″ apart when using yarn, closer when using carpet thread. Pull tight while sewing, but not so tight as to cause puckers or overlapping. Sections should just meet and should lie smoothly next to each other.

Before lacing crocheted or knitted rugs, loop the yarn a couple of times through an outside stitch to secure it. While lacing, take the needle through the loops of the outside stitches. If the rows of stitches run in the same horizontal direction in both sections, align them carefully for joining. Since the joining seams will be visible, you can devise a stitch to be used over them as a decorative feature.

The joining seams will also be visible in flat embroidered rugs, but surface stitches can usually be taken over them to match the rest of the work. If these stitches are large, provisions may have to be made before work begins to leave enough empty area along the edges to accommodate them. On a flat rug it is sometimes better to make the joining seam more pronounced and to include it in the rug design, as in the rug shown on page 31.

For a woven rug or one made on Scandinavian backing, two other stitches can be used. They are variations on the lacing stitch, but they mix or submerge within the filling of the backing so that they are invisible. The first stitch, shown below, is the stronger one of the two and is worked one warp end in from the selvedge. Stitches are spaced ¼″ to ½″ apart. In the second stitch, the stitch is first secured by being looped a couple of times around the selvedge. This stitch is worked close to the selvedge and emerges every ¼″ to ½″ as it moves from one section to the other.

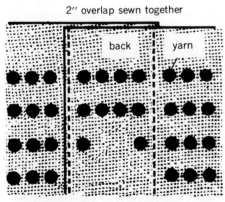

2″ overlap sewn together

back   yarn

Joining widths by overlapping. 2″ overlap for soft backings, less for canvas mesh.

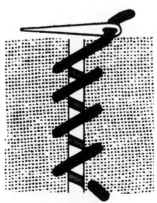

Lacing stitch. Needle goes through space next to edge thread. Pull together so edges meet.

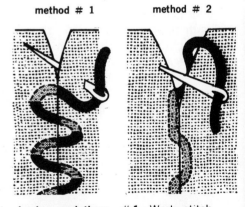

method # 1   method # 2

Lacing variations. #1. Work stitch one warp end in from selvedge. **#2.** Sew stitch through filling alongside selvedge thread.

Fringes

Fringes are either added to the rug or constructed from its body. Purely ornamental, they are meant to enhance the rug aesthetically, and must therefore be considered in relation to the size, pile height, structure, texture, color, and design of the rug. A fringe should not compete with the rug in size or structure, nor should it be skimpy. A rug is a solid piece of textile and demands a sturdy fringe, not a dainty one. If you are unsure about using a fringe, or even about what kind to use, add a bit to the rug to see if the effect pleases you. If it doesn't, try another one, or perhaps tassels at the corners or elsewhere. Unless you feel the fringe complements the rug, its use should be disregarded. At times, however, the right fringe can rescue an otherwise nondescript rug.

You can plan for a fringe beforehand by trying out ideas on your sketch. In this way you can buy yarn for the rug and fringe at the same time. Color and type of yarn will depend on rug texture and color. If the fringe is to hang loose—rather than being braided or knotted for its full length—choose yarn that will not unravel quickly and become stringy.

ATTACHED FRINGES

The examples that follow are simple ways to make the fringe. By experimenting with them you will discover many variations. The yarn is first separated into groups. The number of strands in a group will depend on yarn thickness and on the desired thickness of the fringe. This number will also determine how closely to space the groups when they are pulled through the rug edge and are secured with a holding knot. A group with eight strands, for example, would be spaced farther apart than one with two.

Room has to be left on the rug edge for the fringe to be pulled through. The hem can be made first, and the fringe yarns brought through the double thickness, or the fringe can be attached first and then the hem made. On canvas mesh, leave a row of empty holes. On high pile rugs, leave sufficient space so that the shaggy pile does not hide the fringe. On low pile or flat rugs, attach close to edge so no backing shows through. Since crocheted and knitted rugs do not have a backing, attach the fringe through the space between the first and second rows of stitches. Skip some stitches so the fringe will not be crowded.

Measuring. The finished fringe can be from 2″ to 10″ long. Less than 2″ is too short and more than 10″ becomes a nuisance to keep clean and neat. The cut length is twice the finished length (since the yarn is folded in half), plus 1″ for the knot; add still more to make it easier to knot or braid the fringe. If you plan an intricate fringe, allow additional yarn to compensate for yarn that is taken up in the working process.

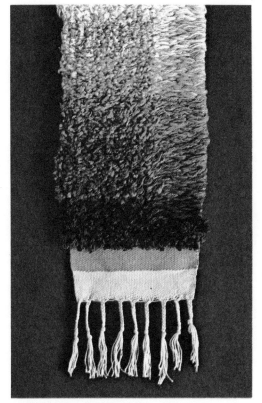

A sampler with braided fringe. In actual rug, the fringe would be next to pile. By Arlene Set.

Fringe is added as rug is being made. Latch-hooked rug by George McGrath.

Starting the fringe. Fold strands of one group in half and pull through rug edge as shown bottom left. Repeat for all groups, spacing them evenly. The fringe can now be knotted or braided.

Knotted fringe. The simplest type of fringe to make is an overhand knot which will secure each group of strands to the rug and allow the ends to hang loose. You can also divide each group in half and knot adjacent halves together (#2, facing page). Push knots up to rug edge to make a tightly crossed effect. Knot the leftover ends of the first and last groups over themselves. Trim loose ends to an even length. For variation, and to keep groups from being too loose, another knot can be made midway, or at the end, of each group. A series of knots can also be made to form a web of crisscrossing groups (#3, facing page). If a wide fringe is to be made, reduce distances between rows—widely spaced areas are easy to trip over.

Braided fringe. Braids can be thick or thin, can continue for the full length of the fringe or stop partway, or can be staggered as in a knotted fringe. For the most part, thick braids look better, and, because of their weight, lie better. Depending on the yarn used, you can double, triple, or quadruple the strands to add thickness. But be careful—too many strands may cause too big a gap between the start of the braid and the rug edge. Pull tight while braiding to minimize this gap and to maintain firmness. Braid as much of the length as you wish and, if quite a bit of fringe is left loose, finish off with an overhand knot. However, if strands are too heavy or there are too many, or if the fringe is too short, this may be too bulky a finishing, and the ends should be whipped instead.

Whipping consists of tightly wrapping a 10″ to 12″ length of yarn around end of braid. Lay 2″ of the yarn in a loop along the area to be whipped, with the loop at the bottom of the braid (#6, facing page). The area covered should be sufficient to thoroughly secure the braid. Usually ½″ is adequate.

SELF-FRINGES
The fringes on woven and braided rugs run across the short, or horizontal, sides only and are made out of the ends of the material that formed the rugs. On a braided rug, machine-stitch across the short sides to keep the rug from coming undone, or else overhand knot the ends. (Although braided rugs are usually not fringed, some rectangular ones can be; see page 76.) A woven rug fringe can be any of the fringes already mentioned. Woven rugs, or those made on Scandinavian backings or any other particularly attractive backings, fall into both the self-fringe and attached fringe categories; provision should be made at the outset to leave enough backing to unravel for a self-fringe. Selvedge edges are left alone.

Before fringing a woven rug, secure the warp and filling by dividing warp ends into groups and knotting each group over itself with an overhand knot. Tie to the filling as closely as possible. Do not include too many ends in one knot since this can cause gaps between the outside ends. To further secure filling, see #7, page 35.

To start fringe

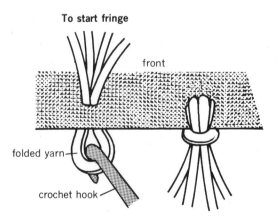

Slip ends through loop to form holding knot and pull tight.

1. Overhand knot.

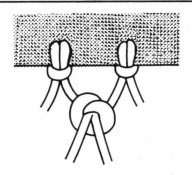

2. Knot adjacent halves of groups together, 1″ below rug edge.

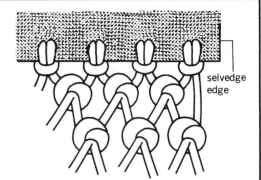

selvedge edge

3. Continue to divide groups, keeping rows at equal distance.

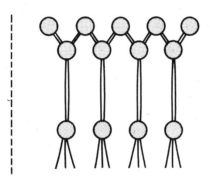

4. Two design variations.

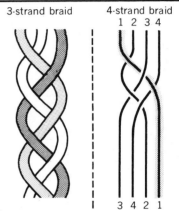

3-strand braid   4-strand braid
1 2 3 4

3 4 2 1

5. For braided fringe. All even- and odd-numbered multiple braids done in same manner as 4-strand.

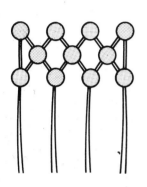

6. Whipping to secure ends. Wrap yarn tightly around braid. Pull beginning end so that loop with tail end is drawn under wrapping (see right). Trim.

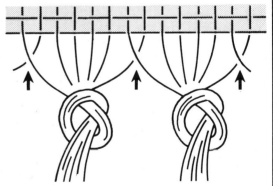

7. To secure filling of woven rugs with overhand knots. Cross edge ends of each group.

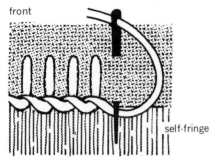

Blanket stitch. Make deep enough to hold filling in.

To fringe a rug made on a backing, first secure rug edge with a blanket stitch (see left). Use either strong yarn or carpet thread in a matching color, or yarn unraveled from the backing. It is easier to do the edge stitch before working on the rug. At least 4″ should be allowed for the fringe. Unravel this amount on all four sides or only on the two short ones (the other two sides will then be hemmed). A knotted or braided fringe can now be made.

Tassels

Tassels are thick groups of yarn about 5″ to 10″ long and at least 1″ in diameter at their bound tops. To make a tassel, cut a piece of wood or cardboard to the length of the desired tassel and wind the yarn around it. Insert an extra length of yarn through one end of the wound group and tie securely. This length will be used to attach the tassel to the rug. Cut the group at the other end. Then whip the uncut end, starting about 1″ or 2″ down from the tied yarn. See Whipping, page 34. (Use a minimum amount of whipping unless it is to be a decorative feature of the tassel.) Insert attaching yarn into rug hem, tie once, and sew down securely on back.

To make a tassel

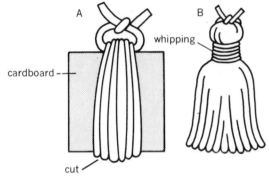

Tassels can be attached at various points on rug edge (see examples below). They can also serve in place of fringes.

Lining

A lining is optional. It serves to lessen wear, acts as a minor cushioning agent, and gives the rug more body. When used, it is usually on a rug with a backing, though crocheted or knitted rugs can also be lined after blocking for further stability. Linings are usually of heavy burlap, heavy-duty denim, serge, cotton rep, or any other closely woven, strong fabric.

Before lining a backed rug, see that the rug hem is made. Cut fabric to rug dimension, plus 1½″ all around for a hem. Pin at intervals to back of rug, starting at the center and working out to the edges,

Three ideas for attaching tassels

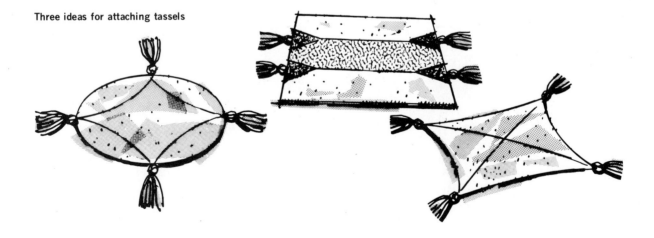

making sure the fit is perfect. Either pin up to the foldline or leave a little rug hem exposed. Sew lining to rug hem with strong thread in a matching color. As a decorative feature, sew an ornamental cross stitch in a contrasting color yarn. Lightly press foldlines.

For a crocheted or knitted rug, cut lining 1″ wider than rug. Turn back a narrow hem so that lining edge lies close to rug edge. Sew directly to the rug with invisible stitches.

Latexing

Latex (a liquid rubber adhesive) is applied to the back of a rug—usually a hooked one—to secure the loops and to provide traction. With tightly packed cut loops, latexing is not necessary; but with continuous rows of uncut loops, there is the chance that a heel could catch in one and pull out a whole row. Various types of latex are available at rug supply and needlework stores. Some have a strong odor, so work with good ventilation. Latex is best spread on with a putty knife or rubber spatula; it can also be painted on with a brush.

To apply, lay the rug face down on a flat surface or, if possible, latex it right on the frame (just be sure it is stretched tight, for if not, any ripples in it will be dried in place). Spread latex on evenly, and so thinly that it just borders on transluscence—if it forms an opaque coat, you have applied too much. If latex is put on thickly or with too much pressure, it might go through to the surface and adhere to the tufts, making them rigid. When spread thinly, a quart can cover an 8′ or 9′ square rug. Some latex will dry in a couple of hours, some overnight, and others will remain tacky for a couple of days.

The latexing on a washable rug will dissolve a little with each washing, but will still give years of service. If you want to skid-proof a rug other than a hooked one, latex edges or corners only.

Rug Corners and Pads

Corners that curl up can be flattened by pressing, or by sewing on lead drapery weights; large rubber triangles, cut out of a carpet pad; or rubber jar rings. The last two also make the rug skid-proof.

In order to protect the rug and preserve its beauty, consider using a rug pad. The pad will give the rug traction, as well as providing a cushion underfoot. You can buy pads in standard rug sizes or have them cut to order; or you can make your own out of heavy felt padding, rubber lining, or foam-rubber sheets. The pad should be ½″ to 1½″ smaller than the rug and not so thick that the rug is visibly raised from the floor. Placing the rug on a large carpet will also help preserve it. However, be sure that the texture and color of rug and carpet complement each other.

Tack lining at intervals to the backing so it will not hang loose.

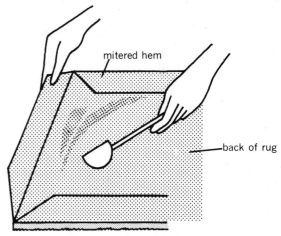

Apply latex to back of hooked rug and press hem down.

Cleaning

With care, your rug can be kept free from dirt and stains and continue to look as good as the day it was put on the floor. Weekly use of a vacuum cleaner will remove surface dirt before it has a chance to become embedded. On occasion, vacuum the underside as well. If the rug is reversible, as are braided ones and most woven, knitted, and crocheted rugs, it should be turned over every so often. Attend to spots and stains while they are fresh and remove as much of them as you can with an absorbent cloth or the edge of a knife, working toward the center of the stain so as not to spread it.

For grease stains, use a dry-cleaning fluid. For food stains (coffee, tea, gravy, milk, chocolate, egg) make a solution of 1 tsp. white vinegar and 1 tsp. soap flakes to 1 qt. cool water. This solution also removes ink and blood stains. Gum, tar, lipstick, and crayon can usually be removed with dry-cleaning fluid; if not, use the solution above. Alcohol, soft drinks, and non-greasy foods can best be removed by sponging with warm water. Repeat if necessary after the initial effort has dried. Brush up pile once it is dry.

If you want to clean the entire rug and brighten its color, there are two possible home-cleaning methods. One is to use a dry powder shampoo and the other is to use a liquid shampoo. Follow manufacturer's directions. Test a patch of the rug for color fastness before shampooing.

Braided rugs can usually be scrubbed quite vigorously. Small knitted or crocheted ones can also be washed like a fine sweater in lukewarm water with a liquid soap like Woolite. Do not rub, just soak and rinse *very* well. The rugs may require repeated rinsing.

Thoroughly dry rug before using. Spread it out flat, preferably out-of-doors. Do not wring out, or hang over a clothesline while wet. The weight of the wet material will either pull the backing out of shape or strain the stitches. Knitted or crocheted rugs should be blocked and dried flat after being rolled in a towel to absorb excess moisture.

The flexible rug beater that was common not so long ago is still an excellent means of beating dirt out of a rug. If you are lucky enough to have one, use it on the back of the rug so that you beat the dust and dirt *out* of the rug and not into it. A coarse, sturdy rug can be thoroughly swept with a whisk broom. Fine embroidered rugs should be beaten (but not too vigorously), then gone over with a clothes brush and wiped clean with a damp cloth.

In general, the vigor of the cleaning should be suited to the technique and the materials in the rug. To heighten the sheen and color in pile rugs, brush with the nap or across it, not against it. Textured, rya, or shag rugs are very effective at hiding dirt and looking clean—but don't be deceived by this: give the rug the cleaning it deserves.

A creative use of different pile heights. Here rya and flossa are combined. Shown in detail above and full rug below. 32″ × 66″. By Michelle Lester.

Repair and Salvage

Tears and frays, once started, can progress quickly if neglected, so it is best to repair damage as soon as it is detected. Mend as invisibly as possible. If the rug has faded, you may have to tone down (by dyeing) the colors you will be using for the repairs.

If some of the rug backing has worn away, cut another piece large enough to extend at least 1″ beyond the edges of the repair area. Position it on the worn spot and baste in place. The patch for an embroidered or latch-hooked rug has to match the original backing thread for thread and hole for hole since the stitches taken through it will have to line up correctly with the original ones. It is not necessary to be that precise with a hooked rug, for the nature of the craft is such that the patch does not have to be aligned thread for thread, nor do the loops have to be the same pattern as before.

Flat embroidered rugs. After the patch is basted in place, turn rug face up and cut away frayed edges and badly worn parts of the backing. Allow some worn stitches around a patch to remain, for they can serve as padding for the new ones. Overcast backing to patch around cutout area so it will not shift as you put in the stitches. Embroider over three or four rows of worn or flattened stitches, but forego this if, by so doing, this area will be raised above others. The new stitches should completely conceal the patch, and must match the old stitches in technique, color, and materials.

To finish off, turn rug face down. If backing is pliable enough, turn raw edges of patch under and sew them close to the new stitches. If not, cut away excess and sew raw edges to backing. Place a damp cloth over patch and press with a fairly hot iron.

If you are lucky enough to have only worn stitches, with the backing still intact, just pull out the weakest ones and redo them with fresh yarn over the remaining worn ones.

You can conceal a tear by sewing its torn edges together on the back and redoing the embroidery stitches on the front. You can also use a decorative stitch that is different than the others, but it should look as if its purpose is purely ornamental. A patch is necessary for really bad tears.

Pile rugs. Embroidered rya rugs, latch-hooked rugs, and other high pile rugs rarely need repairs (the underside is well protected by the pile), but if they should, then repair them as described above —except remove all frayed knots since you could not very well stitch over them.

Pile that is badly crushed, but not worn, can be revived by steaming (page 30). Do *not* press. Brush pile briskly. Repeat treatment until effects of crushing have disappeared. Shag combs or rakes are available in department stores to comb out and revive flattened rya pile.

Contrasting materials add textural interest. In detail above, rug below, handspun wool is mixed with black karakul. 60″ × 82″. By Nell Scott.

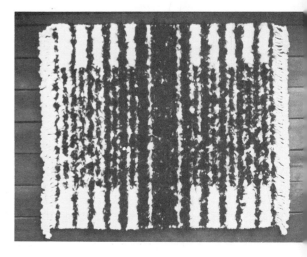

Hooked rugs. If the backing is worn, prepare a patch as above and pin or baste it in place. Depending on size and location of worn area, repair the rug in hand or stretch it on a frame. With rug face up, overcast backing to patch. Pull out a few hooked loops around it and mix them in with the new materials that will be used; this will help overcome any color difference. Hook through both layers of backing to make a neater finish on the underside and to doubly secure the patch. The patch should be secure with the hooking, but you can also finish off as in the embroidered rug. Tears are best fixed with a patch.

If just some pile has worn away, simply pull out what worn stitches remain and rehook with fresh materials. If the edge rows of hooking are frayed, take worn rows out and turn backing under to rows that are intact. Then re-hem or re-bind. A worn backing edge can be strengthened by being bound with rug tape or by having a braid attached. One or two braids, each ¾″ wide, can be sewn around the perimeter of the rug. These braids, though functional in purpose, should be treated as decorative additions and should work well with the color and design of the rug. A badly worn edge can be replaced by sewing a new strip of backing along the entire length or width of the underside of the rug and then hooking through it. The strip should be wide enough to allow at least 2″ for a hem. Overcast cut edges and join by overlapping and sewing through quite securely.

If the rug is round or oval it will not be possible to use a straight strip of backing because it will buckle, as will a bias strip. Instead, a series of step-like patches, of the same backing material, will have to be attached. The weave of these patches should travel in the same direction as the old backing. Cut patches on the bias, overlap edges, and sew on to rug backing. Hook where necessary. Cut off excess material so that a hem margin conforming to rug's outline is left. Turn back and sew.

Crocheted and knitted rugs. If the rug was made in strips or in small sections joined together, try to repair damage with needle or matching thread. If you can't, then undo joining seams and remove worn portion. Do a new area and rejoin. It is difficult to repair a rug that was done in one piece, but with patience you may be able to simulate the stitch.

Braided rugs. If a length of braid is worn, remove it and sew new strips of material to the braid ends that the original length had been sewn to. Braid the strips, then lace and butt (see page 79) in place. If outer braids are worn, simply remove them and substitute new ones in their place.

Woven rugs. If a warp end breaks or wears away, a new one can be inserted and woven into the filling. It must be knotted to a still sturdy section of the old end. Conceal the knot in the filling and pull the new end as taut as the other warp ends. If the areas of filling need to be replaced, weave them in as invisibly as possible.

This rug is not only excitingly shaped, but it combines materials and techniques as well. It is made of cowhair, linen, and Mexican handspun wool, worked in a flatweave with rya knots. "Shaped Rug #1," by Cynthia Schira. 35″ × 60″.

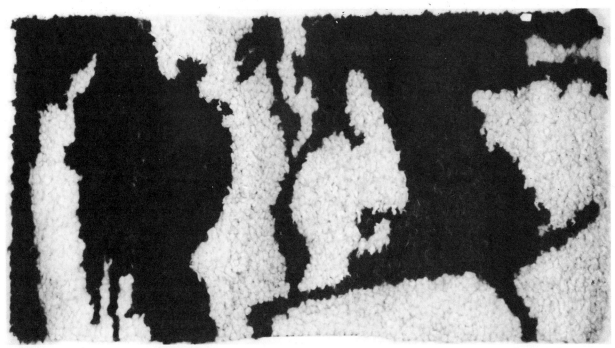

Rugs can also be used to decorate a wall. Example is rya rug by Glen Kaufman.

Worn pile can be taken out and new knots easily inserted. If selvedge edges are frayed, work over them with a blanket stitch (page 58) in colors to match the filling. Badly worn edge warp ends can sometimes be made into a fringe after enough filling has been removed. (Fringe the other end also so that both ends match.) Or, instead of a fringe, the edge can be bound and hemmed once enough filling has been taken out and the ends knotted and trimmed.

If the rug is so badly worn that only a few good portions are left, salvage these to bind and use as chair seats or mats, or to cover footstools. Or use one as the starting point for a new rug—perhaps as the center for a braided, crocheted, or knitted one. Be sure that the new technique looks well with the old piece and that color, design, and texture are compatible.

STORAGE

Ideally, a rug should be stored flat, but since this is often impossible, the next best way is to roll it, preferably around a pole, face side in. Usually one is cautioned to roll a hooked rug face out because otherwise the backing might weaken and possibly split. However, so long as the backing is of good quality, a hooked rug can be rolled in the same manner as any other.

Before storing a rug, vacuum it thoroughly, back and front. Then spray with a moth spray, taking care that it penetrates deep into the pile. Wrap in heavy brown paper, plastic bags, or a sheet. There should be no holes in the wrapping, and it should be securely attached to the rug so no moths can possibly enter. As a final precaution, store in a place that is neither too hot nor too dry.

Design

Designing a rug is not difficult—even those who say they cannot draw a straight line have found they can participate fully in this absorbing, stimulating, and satisfying area of rugmaking. Offered here are aids to help you understand design so that you can have the personal gratification of executing your own ideas.

A RUG IN THE ROOM

Unless you are motivated solely by the desire to design and make a rug, and its end use is not a dominant consideration, you should give some thought to where the rug will be placed and to the color scheme, mood, or style of its surroundings. The following are points to consider:

1. Rug size can make a room appear larger or smaller or change its proportions completely. If the rug is too small for the room, it can seem as isolated as a stamp on a large envelope; if too large, too rich in texture, too bright in color, or too bold in design, it can seem to be bursting beyond the room's boundaries. Consider rug size and proportion in terms of the furniture that will be placed on or around the rug, as well as the location of doors, windows, or fireplaces. To test for size, you can cut various lengths and widths out of newspapers or wrapping paper and position them on the floor.

2. A rug can divide space by defining a conversational grouping or a dining area. It can pull various elements of a room together. Or it can be a focal point of activity and visual attention.

3. The design and shape of a rug can direct traffic. However, if the rug will receive too much traffic or soil, either alter its position or move furniture to change traffic patterns. Dark or medium colors stay fresh-looking longer while light colors are early victims to soot and grime. Very dark colors show lint and dust quickly. A high-pile rug, a patterned rug, or one combining two or three colors will not show dirt as readily as a flat rug in a solid color.

4. Consider what the rug will be resting on. If on a wood, brick, or tile floor, will the colors be compatible? If on carpeting, it is best to have a strong textural contrast (such as a shag rug on a very low, tightly looped carpet), particularly if the colors are close.

5. Textural quality also decides placement. Rya rugs that are pleasant under bare feet are good for bedrooms and children's rooms, while shorter piles or tighter loops are best for hallway or foyer.

6. Mood is an indefinite quality that a rug can contribute to or can create. Color, texture, and design can impart a quiet, peaceful mood or a dramatic, striking one. An informal mood is associated with braided, flatweave, or rya rugs; a formal one with low pile, loop, or embroidered rugs. Symmetrically placed geometrics in medium color tones usually contribute to a sedate and conservative mood.

This rug, with its three levels of pile, was inspired by the architecture on an island in Greece. "Kalymnos," by Nell Znamierowski.

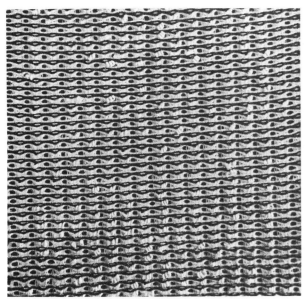

(Above) A rug to complement a setting. Allover-patterned rug woven of sisal, jute, and cotton by Ida Dean Grae. Photo by Hans J. Schiller.

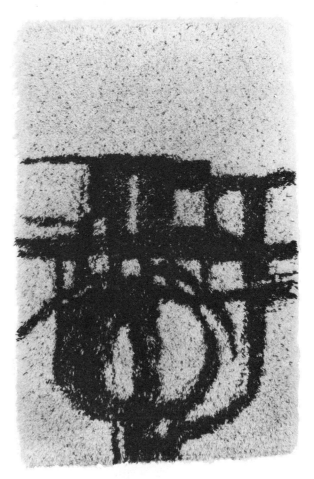

(Right) A rug as a focal point. "Construction," by Sirpa Yarmolinsky. 43″ × 68″. Photo by Day Walters.

(Below) A deep-piled rug in rich colors can spark up a room. "Chartes II," embroidered by Nell Znamierowski.

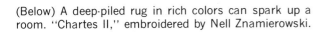

7. Color is often the unifying element in a room of many styles or patterns. View colors under the same light the rug will be exposed to. Colors look different under sunlight, direct or diffused light, fluorescent, white, yellow, rose, or blue light. Bright colors help dimly lit rooms or those with little sunlight. To stress sunlight, use yellow or orange-yellow shades. Pale colors require less light than dark ones since they reflect light, while dark ones absorb it.

Design Considerations

If you question your designing ability, think of the early American rugmakers: they had something to communicate and did so, each according to his ability. The rugs they designed are humble, sincere, and unique, and the charm they impart has nothing to do with whether or not they were made by artists.

Your surroundings. Interesting form is all around us, and becoming aware of it is the first step in learning design. Such casual patterns as the composition of tools scattered on a counter or the arrangement of containers on a shelf are studies for design ready to be seen and interpreted, as are tree branches and leaves outlined against the sky or the shadow patterns cast by a fire escape.

Once you become sensitive to your surroundings, you will begin thinking of applying a seen impression to a rug design. Jot that idea down on paper. You can rearrange it until it suits you and then use it as the basis for a full-size or scale drawing (page 26). In the initial stages, there can be much discarding of ideas and trying of others. None of this is wasted effort, for with every sketch something is learned, and perhaps the seed of the next design planted. What is important is that you have begun to design.

Guidelines. The sketches need not be literal translations of what you see. You can use symbols such as lines, circles, or squares to indicate where parts of the design are to fall. Then once you have the basics of your pattern, you can begin adding color. In essence you will be creating abstract art, which is a more direct and simple way of looking at the world around us. If you should ever be at a loss for a design idea, ask a child to draw a picture for you—the directness with which children view their surroundings usually results in uncomplicated abstract drawings.

A guideline for your first design is *keep it simple*. To try a complex Oriental rug design might seem a challenge, but it is one best left to a second or third rug. Executing a simple design will help you learn the rug technique chosen and will not leave you with the

An example of a strong directional design. Hooked rug, 35″ × 60″, by Marla Mallett.

(Facing page) A deep pile adds depth and dimension to a rug. "Alone," by Uhra Simberg-Ehrström. Courtesy of The Finnish National Tourist Office.

DESIGN INTERPRETATION

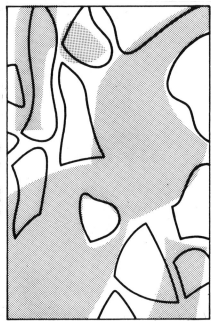

1. A simple and common natural setting. Photo by Glenn Winchester.

2. A line adaptation with color added.

3. A freer adaptation.

feeling of defeat that might follow if you were to attempt too intricate a pattern. If the design you have done is too busy, edit it—take out what seems too much for your eye. If there are too many lines and shapes going in every direction, eliminate some of them until you achieve the right sense of balance. To see how this principle works, it would be helpful to take a postcard or magazine reproduction of a well-known work, or an advertisement or photograph that you find pleasing, and, using tracing paper, draw in the main areas or lines that pull your eye into the work. Also, by repeating forms or lines a sense of rhythm can be created.

Before you get too involved with making that rose look as if you could smell it, take a look at the work of Persian artisans and note that, although every flower and animal can be recognized, they are simple, stylized versions of the real thing. Also keep in mind that although yarn or fabric give texture and life to a pattern, if the pattern is too busy, and there are too many different textures, the result may be muddled.

A simple beginning design can be a repeat motif—that is, one motif (or more than one) repeated over and over to create a pattern. (Examples are given on pages 66, 68, and 85.) If the rug technique you have chosen requires a backing, you can design large motifs, cut their shapes out of sturdy paper, and arrange them on the backing until you are satisfied with their placement (see page 27). Then pin them down and outline their shapes with a felt-tipped pen.

Color

Color is perhaps the most fascinating element in rugmaking. It can be the single item that effects perfect harmony between the rug and other colors in the room, even though those colors are different, *or* it can cause so unpleasant and jarring a note as to make you want to hide the rug in a dark closet. Color is an emotional experience, and as such is largely intuitive, but there are guidelines for those who need a helping hand with their color schemes.

Categories. Every color belongs to one of seven categories: *black, white, gray, hue, tint, tone,* or *shade.* For the breakdown of a color into these categories, see triangle on page 48, top.

To sharpen your color perception, look around as you read this and try to put each color you see into one of those categories. Do the same with the clothes you are wearing or with the rugs shown in this book. When colors get close to the gray side of the triangle, it may be difficult to pinpoint them exactly, but if you can begin to separate tints, tones, and shades, you will soon understand how colors are formed.

Characteristics. Every color has three characteristics: *hue,* the name of a color family (as well as color at its purest and brightest); *value,* the amount of white or black in a color; and *intensity* (or *chroma*), the amount of brightness or dullness in a color, measured by the color's distance from gray. A color has these three characteristics in varying amounts. For example, a deep wine color might belong to the red *hue* family, be of dark *value,* and have little *intensity.* Look again at the colors around you and check for these characteristics.

Color wheel. Fashion writers have given so many names to a single color that its true identity can be obscured, but if we know its position on a color wheel its name becomes relatively unimportant. The wheel (page 48) was drawn to show the major color divisions. Using this wheel as a guide, you can make your own with yarns and fabric scraps; the positioning of the scraps will be determined by the amount of red, yellow, or blue each contains. There should be a smooth transition throughout the wheel.

Simultaneous contrast. Of all the laws or principles governing color, this is one that I believe to be supreme since it regulates how the eye reacts to color placement. It clearly demonstrates how colors are affected by their neighbors. One of the noteworthy aspects of simultaneous contrast is that once you understand it, you can make a rug with a limited palette. By successfully mixing colors and placing them in constantly different positions in relationship to one another, the color range will appear quite large.

Two colors spaced apart may give the eye one impression, but when placed next to each other their individual values, hues, and intensities readjust and give quite a different impression. That skein of yarn you fell in love with may lose some of its charm when mixed

A rug of many colors. "Kungsgatan," by Naomi Towner.

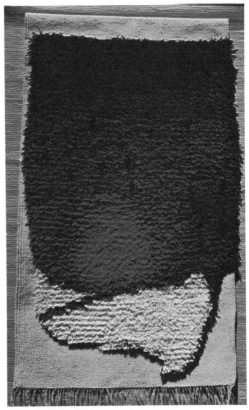

A monochromatic rug (different shades of the same hue). By Anne Hornby.

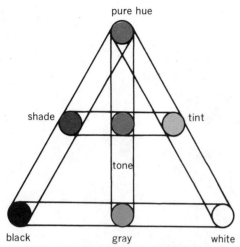

The 7 categories of a color. Hue is color at its purest and brightest. Tint is the mixture between hue and white; tone, between hue and gray; and shade, between hue and black.

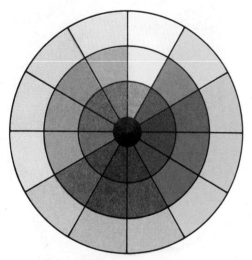

Color wheel. Primary colors are yellow, red, and blue. The secondary colors are between them. Outer ring shows a tint of the hue; middle ring, pure hue; and inner ring, a shade of the hue.

with the other colors of the rug. However, a color that is influenced unfavorably by one neighbor can often be saved by being repositioned next to a friendlier one.

Since color is not always what it appears to be, how then can we be sure of it? One way is by experimenting to see how colors interact. The experiments can be quite modest, and are best done with yarn or fabric since this is what the rug will be composed of. But chips of color cut from magazines can also serve this purpose, as can working to scale on a sheet of paper with felt-tipped pens, crayons, or paints. You can draw blocks or lines of color (see diagrams, facing page). White is the best background to use since it is a common denominator against which all colors retain their true hue. Be careful to have the colors right up against each other or else the experiments will suggest false conclusions. You can then test these colors against the background the rug will actually be resting on. In experimenting, you might want to try some of the harmonies shown (bottom of facing page), any of which would make a suitable color combination for a rug.

Besides determining the overall color effect, consider color in small areas. Here the beginner could make a rug sampler to see how a one-color effect is achieved by combining many colors. The resulting color will be intense if the materials are similar in hue, value, and intensity, but the effect will be peppered if the materials differ greatly in these characteristics. To see how well this color mixing works, I recommend studying two sources—Scandinavian rya rugs and French Impressionist paintings.

Scandinavian ryas have a diffused color quality partially achieved by mixing many colors in a single knot. Solid color in large areas is broken up and made subtle by the fall of the high cut pile. The pile also casts shadows which create changes in color.

The paintings of the French Impressionists have much to do with the formulation of present-day color theory, particularly in their use of the technique called pointillism—a one-color effect obtained by the use of many colors. In a painting, this effect is like reflected sunshine, but if one looks closely, it can be seen that the vibrancy is caused by a visual mixing of complementary colors.

Complementary contrast falls within the principle of simultaneous contrast. When complements (the colors directly opposite each other on the color wheel) are placed next to each other they retain their true hue and stimulate each other to maximum vividness. (This is assuming that they are used in rather good-sized areas and are equal in proportion, value, and intensity.)

In an Oriental rug, color and design are in total harmony. One can easily imagine how some of these ornate patterns would look if they were not so well balanced or if the colors were not so well planned. The nature of the design is to break up solid color areas so that few are left. This means that a color does not have a totality all its own but has instead an intertwined relationship with other

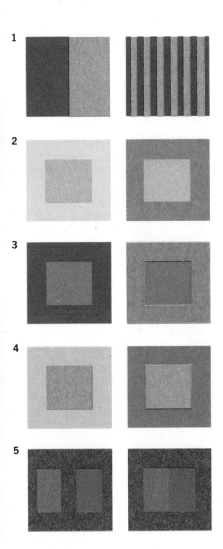

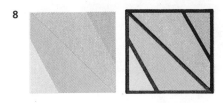

COLOR RELATIONSHIPS

1. Complements mixed equally in small areas create a gray effect.

2. A medium value looks darker on a light background and lighter on a dark one.

3. A bright color will appear even brighter, or duller, depending on adjacent color.

4. A hue will tend toward being more blue, red, or yellow depending on adjacent color.

5. Closely related colors can appear alike depending on background.

6. Some colors may sink into the background so that they lose subtle differences.

7. The color used in larger proportion has more influence than one used in a lesser amount.

8. Fine black lines around color will heighten and define it.

9. Limited color palette for maximum color effect. **A.** Two colors give six effects. **B.** Three colors give a multi-colored effect.

COLOR HARMONIES

A. Monochromatic—tones, tints, and shades of a hue.

B. Analogous—adjacent colors on the color wheel.

C. Complementary—opposite colors on color wheel.

D. Split complementary—a color with two colors adjoining its complement.

E. Triad—three colors, a uniform number of steps removed from each other on color wheel.

F. Tetrad—four colors, three steps removed from one another on color wheel.

colors in the rug. A solid color effect is usually achieved through the intermingling of many colors. The borders are not harsh separations from the center of the rug since, again through distribution of color, the impact of background colors is distilled. Oriental artisans outlined the colors, so that if you closely observe a small area you will see that the colors stand out like jewels or look constantly different if the outlines used are of various colors.

Through experimenting to find the right proportions and combinations, you will achieve confidence as well as greater control over colors. If you are at a loss as to what colors to choose, pick those you like or experiment with those you are hesitant about. Most of the mistakes that occur in choosing rug colors fall on the side of timidity. Try the unusual or vivid. Don't be afraid to change the colors or their placement if they seem out of harmony with the room. If you are experimenting with new colors, give them a chance. As you see the colors in the room over a period of time, you may find that the more exotic hues or combinations you once thought were too rich to live with have become quite natural to have around. Remember that color should always be selected with the nature of the material in mind. Collecting snips of color in different textures of yarn and fabric will enable you to see how texture alters color. A knowledge of color will be an invaluable asset if you decide to dye your own materials.

(Above) A split complementary color scheme is dominant in this hooked rug by Marla Mallett.

(Right) An example of an analogous color scheme with the complement red as an accent. Hooked by Barbara Factor.

Texture

Texture is as much an element of design as is a shape or a line. Unless you are following the dictates of a special design or color combination, it will often be the texture of the material that will first excite you and that will make you want to use it, thereby dictating how the color choices will be made and how the pattern will be structured.

A rug that combines different textures, even though in one color or in subdued colors, can spark up a room. By taking advantage of texture, straight lines can be softened and warmth added to what might otherwise be a cold interior—especially if there is much use of plastic, glass, or metal in the furnishings.

Pile of various heights can add interest and excitement to a solid-color rug. Different levels of pile give a sculptured effect to the rug and create patterns as well. The interest can also be in the combination of uncut (loop) and cut pile, or in the mixture of a variety of textured yarns or fabrics. (The pile length reflects light differently than the cut tip.)

There are many raw materials that can be worked with, and you should study all that are available to see how you respond to the textural qualities of these materials. Once you do respond to a particular material, you will then find ways to utilize its best or most interesting qualities.

The use of hard twist yarns with soft (almost roving) types, dull yarns with shiny ones, and fine yarns with heavy ones will add contrast, as well as interest, whether the rug is a flatweave or a low or high pile rug. A highly textured fabric like corduroy can be imagined in combination with a very flat satin or cotton cloth. An accent of "silky" yarns can lend a luxurious quality to a short pile rug. The greatest amount of textural interest is in a high pile rug with a mixture of materials. In some techniques, yarns and fabrics can be combined to good advantage. Each technique also creates its own texture—a crocheted rug, for example, has a different texture than one that is braided or hooked.

Just about any material (so long as it is comfortable to walk on) can be used in a rug. Such yarns as mohair loop or a fine bouclé would be obvious exceptions. The ancient Chinese and Persians used silk and gold threads in their rugs, and as long ago as 2000 B.C. when pile carpets were a sophisticated art form, there were other craftsmen who made carpets out of felt. They would then applique them with figures cut out of leather which they had dyed.

There are many other possibilities for the imaginative use of materials. Felt, raffia, cord, string, jute, vinyl, leather, and fur are just a few of the materials that can be explored for added textural effect. At present they are not being used extensively and therefore offer great potential for experimentation.

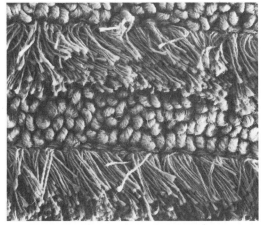

Alternating rows of short loop and long cut pile. By Ida D. Grae. Photo by Hans J. Schiller.

An even surface of cut and loop pile.

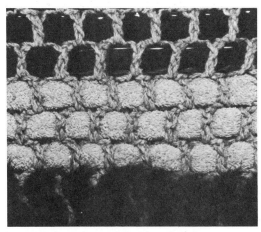

Interweaving of a variety of materials.

Dyeing

Home dyeing is often the answer when the color you want is not available in stores or when you wish to change or soften the color of materials you have at home. It is also the only way to achieve certain effects and shadings. As you experiment with different dyeing methods, keep in mind that dyeing is an adventure and that you should not be upset if colors come out differently than expected—they can surprise you by looking lovely when worked into the rug.

Since most material appears darker when wet (deep values will show little difference), test for the right shade by taking a paper towel or an old cloth towel and blotting a corner of the fabric or a few inches of the yarn until dry. If you are matching to a color on a chart, remember that with some colors the result may be only a reasonable likeness since printer's ink and dye differ, as do fiber and paper.

There are two kinds of dye—the commercial, available in stores or from dyehouses; and the natural or vegetable, obtained from plants. The commercial dyes will be discussed here, and recommended books on natural dyes are in the bibliography at the end of this book. Some pointers to go by when home dyeing follow.

DYEING METHODS

Dyeing unbleached or white material. This is the surest way to get a true color since there is no dye in the material to affect the new one. For a soft tone, add a pinch of gray or the color's complement.

Overdyeing. To deepen or brighten a hue, dye over it with the same color or with one of the same family. A complement will gray the color. A weak bath of gray or the color's complement or of an extremely weak black will often soften a dyed color. Overdyeing gray or beige results in a soft tone. Overdyeing can produce interesting color combinations on tweed fabrics and heather yarns and on patterns such as checks and stripes. When a group of colors do not relate, or when you want subtle nuances of one color from an assortment of many, immerse in a weak bath of the desired hue or in the complement most common to all.

Piece dyeing. Different fibers absorb dye in varying degrees. Immersing them in a common dye bath will result in variegated shades.

Spot dyeing. Another way to obtain variegated color is to sprinkle material with bleach. For soft shading, crowd material into dye bath and either do not stir often or sprinkle with concentrated dye of almost paste consistency. For strong mottling, dissolve dye with water and splash over material with a spoon. Have material quite wet if you want the dye to spread; if not, keep it dry. Various colors can be put on. Sprinkle salt liberally over material, place in a large, flat pan with 1″ of boiling water, and simmer, covered, for ½ hour. Stir occasionally so material will not scorch.

EQUIPMENT

Soap flakes—use soft water.

Large pan—use as dye pot. Enamel, stainless steel, or copper.

Wooden or glass rods or spoons—to lift materials and stir dye bath. Chopsticks or metal tongs can also be used.

Pan—for rinsing.

Glass measuring cup—to mix dye concentrate in. Use a large container if you want to dilute concentrate.

Common salt—to exhaust bath after dyeing.

Glass jars with lids—to store dye bath or concentrate.

Cloth-lined rubber gloves

Cover-all apron

Dip dyeing. For various tints of the same color, use one bath; for a multi-hued effect, use several different baths. Dip one end of skein or fabric into bath, then dip another section, and continue in this manner until all the material is dyed.

Tie dyeing. This is another way to get different colors in the material. Tie off areas with cord or rubber bands so that the dye will not penetrate. Remove them after dyeing. The undyed areas can then be dyed a different shade or left as is.

Bleaching. Partial bleaching can mute or lighten very dark colors. This is sometimes accomplished, depending on color and fiber content, by lengthy soaking in hot water and strong soap. Boiling takes more color out. For stronger results, try color remover, following package directions, or household bleach. But use with great care, so that the fiber is not destroyed in the process. Rinse thoroughly.

Overdyeing with black. If you did not get the desired color, you can overdye with black. Whether a true black will result depends on the previous color. Adding a little of the color's complement may help.

DYEING PROCEDURE

1. Cut or tear fabric into manageable pieces. Put yarn into skeins and tie loosely so they will not tangle but dye can penetrate. Then wash material in hot water and soap flakes to remove surface dirt and yarn oil. Soak while dye bath is being prepared. Note: If material had been washed previously, wet thoroughly in medium-hot water and a *small* amount of soap flakes.

2. Have enough water in the dye pot to cover material. Make dye concentrate according to package instructions, add to water, and mix thoroughly. Rinse material to remove most of the soap, but not all. This will help the dye to penetrate faster. Wring out material and put into barely simmering dye bath. Do not crowd; the material should have plenty of room to move around so that dyeing will be even.

3. Lift and stir alternately to keep material constantly moving. With the commonly used dyes, usually the longer the material remains in the bath, the deeper the color will be; for lighter tone, leave in only a short time. With dyes from dye houses, light tints can sometimes be achieved by immersion in a bath that has already been used to dye material to full strength.

4. When most of the color has left the bath, remove material and add a handful to a ½ cup of salt (amount varies according to amount of material). Stir to dissolve and put material back in. By adding salt you assure that the dye will adhere to the material, and that the bath will be exhausted of any dye left in it.

5. Remove material. Hold over bath until dripping has stopped. Rinse in successively cooler baths; the first should be almost the temperature of the dye bath, and the last cool to cold. (By the last bath the water should be absolutely clear.) Squeeze out water, but do not wring, and hang material to dry.

A common dye bath unifies patterned fabrics for use in a rug.

Commercially-dyed colors that clash with home-dyed ones can be softened by overdyeing. Detail of braided rug by Shirley Sayles.

(Above) Gorse blooming in Donegal was inspiration for woven rug by Doris Clement.

(Right) "Eternity," by Nell Znamierowski. Suggested by border design at bottom of facing page.

(Below) Unusual photographs provide ready-made ideas for rugs.

Sources of Inspiration

When you begin designing rugs you will soon become a collector of yarn or fabric strips, of color and design ideas, or of whatever else you feel may at some time become the basis for a pattern. This collection is one of the sources you can draw upon whenever the time is ripe for another rug.

Another is the natural environment, whether viewed firsthand or through photographs; it is the greatest storehouse for ideas, literal or abstract. Trips to a botanical garden or a zoo, going on a hike, or just browsing through a seed catalogue or nature magazine can provide endless inspiration. Museums are another good source—they house countless motifs and shapes that can be interpreted with very little effort on the viewer's part. Or you may find that the drapery, upholstery, or furniture that will accompany the rug contains a curve or line or some bit of pattern that can be used as the start of a design idea.

Inspiration is an individual matter; it can happen casually or it may require concentrated research. Perhaps the following sources for design ideas will help stimulate you.

Travel—whether you go on a brief trip or around the world, you are going to see something new. It is a good idea to collect postcards and booklets on route. Also, you can make shorthand sketches to refer to when you are home again.

Calligraphy—for the really personal touch, try entwining your initials into an artful pattern, or use Arabic or Oriental letters.

Stained glass windows—their self-contained round or rectangular shapes are readymade sources for interpretation.

Historical motifs—choose an event or period in history that has caught your imagination and research it in libraries or museums. Gravestone rubbings or carvings on antiques are other sources. The motifs on old plates make interesting round rug patterns.

Fantasy—children's books are a good source, especially those with simple drawings and shapes.

Symbolism—a rug design can be inspired by symbols or signs from ritual, magic, and astrology. Hex signs are a good source.

Mythology—examples from the ancient Egyptians, Greeks, and Romans can be found in their pottery, coins, mosaics, jewelry, tomb paintings, and marble carvings.

Shapes—geometric shapes provide simple backgrounds for color and texture interplay. Technology has provided further patterns; some can be seen in transistor panels or on computer cards.

Free forms—interesting free-form patterns can come into being by folding a sheet of paper several times and letting a pair of scissors practically guide itself as it cuts.

Chinese pillar rug, late 19th century. Courtesy of The Textile Museum Collection, Washington, D.C.

A delight in discovery awaits you once you are able to visualize a rug design from a source of inspiration. Some sources can be translated almost literally—such as the three examples below of weathered barn wood, gold jewelry, and a wood carving. Also shown is a Peruvian example of a butterfly theme adapted from nature. Still other themes can be seen in the four rugs on the facing page.

Adapting from nature: Butterfly motif. Peru, 15th century. The Cooper-Hewitt Museum of Decorative Arts and Design, Smithsonian Institution.

SOME SOURCES OF INSPIRATION

Weathered barn wood. Suggests a textural design. Photo by Ned Harris.

Detail of gold jewelry suggests high and low pile.

Decorative wood carving. A repeat motif.

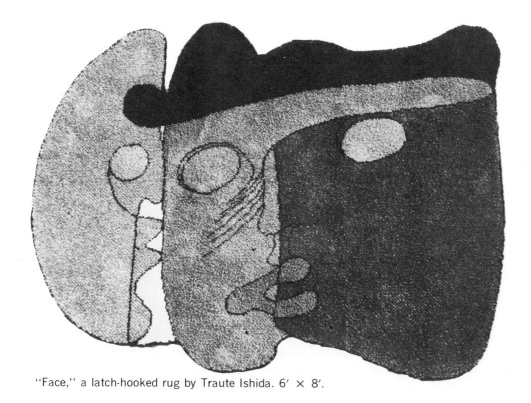

"Face," a latch-hooked rug by Traute Ishida. 6' × 8'.

"Yellow Ovoids," detail, by Babro Nilsson. The Cooper-Hewitt Museum, Smithsonian Institution.

A household item can suggest a design. "Hourglass," by Cynthia Schira.

"Nude," by Elisabeth af Kleen. 23" × 39". Photo by La Grua Studio.

EDGING STITCHES

Blanket stitch

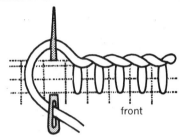

Needle front to back with thread under needle. Pull to shut loop. Move to left and repeat.

Braid stitch

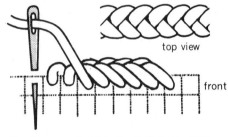

Needle moves back to front. Pull up, move 1 hole to left (¼″ on soft backing), catch tail. Return to start. Move 3 holes left, then back 2. Continue forward 3, back 2.

To end yarn

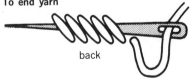

Catching tail at end of stitch.

Embroidery

Most embroidery stitches will produce smooth-faced flat rugs, but textural variation and raised effects can be obtained by using a variety of stitches, or by padding, or by putting in pile areas.

Tools. Large-eyed needle (I prefer a thick, blunt tapestry, rug, or rya needle). Optional: Automatic yarn cutter, yarn or pile gauge (page 18). Frame (see page 24) for stretching work taut (not necessary with canvas mesh).

Backings. Rug warp cloth, canvas mesh, or others (see pages 22–23).

Materials. Rug yarn, used singly or in a group (three strands are sufficient for a group, but four or five can be used). With canvas mesh, yarn thickness must be in proportion to the number of holes per inch, otherwise the backing will not be fully covered (the lower the hole count, the thicker the yarn). With more closely woven backings, yarn thickness is determined by the length and density of the planned stitch. Note: Fabric strips, ½″ wide (knits are best), can be used in place of yarn.

DESIGN AND DIMENSIONS

Small, intricate patterns are best left for the flat stitches, and bold, simple ones for pile areas. Stitches can be brought into sharper relief by being worked over padding (see Gobelin stitch, page 61). Try to have padding the same color as the stitch. Use thick, soft yarn or soft fabric strips (flannel is good).

Rug shape and dimension can be whatever you wish. With canvas mesh, however, a beginner might find it difficult to turn a hem on a shape other than rectangular (see diagram, page 29).

A beginner transferring a design to canvas mesh will find it easiest to make a full-size drawing (page 26). However, if graph paper is used instead, I suggest that each square equal one hole in the mesh, though you can, of course, set up your own gauge. For other backings, use any means of transferring.

BEFOREHAND PREPARATIONS

Allow for a 1½″ to 2″ hem on the backing. If you plan to work selvedge to selvedge, allow ½″. Cut yarn into 20″ to 30″ lengths, but not longer. Longer lengths tangle too easily. Thread the yarn or yarn groups. If different colors are used, they can be threaded beforehand to save time. If there will be many color changes, use five or six needles, a different one for every color.

You have to decide at the outset whether to turn the hem before or after making the rug (see page 28). If done before, edging stitches are taken on the foldline to form an attractive frame for the work and to keep the hem folded. Fairly thick wool or synthetic yarn in a color coordinated with the design is recommended. Do not make edging deeper than the second hole in from the fold on canvas mesh, or more than ½″ in on other backings. A crocheted edging

Contemporary rug made by Arabs in Israel. Lined with material from tents. Uses cross stitch and tent stitch. Collection of Mr. and Mrs. Steve Manville.

of heavy yarn can be made instead. On Scandinavian backing, stitch non-selvedge edges only. If you plan a fringe, *do not* put on edging, but leave a space or a row of holes (depending on backing) to attach the fringe. For a Swedish braid or for a self-fringe on Scandinavian backing, leave an extra 4″ which can be unraveled.

Suggested for edging are the blanket or braid stitches (left). When working braid stitches around a corner, shorten the stitch preceding a corner by going into the second hole instead of the third. If you are working on soft backing, or if you are an accomplished stitcher, you will be able to make easy turnings with few if any compensations.

TECHNIQUE

You may want to work one color at a time, thereby skipping to various parts of the design, but until you gain experience it is better to work in small areas, going row by row. Keep stitches short and compact; long, loose ones are apt to catch or rub up. Do not pull stitches too tight; those with a slight give cover the backing more fully, wear longer, and are more resilient to walk on. As a beginner it is best to cut the thread at the end of each row and begin anew. When starting or finishing a strand, leave a 1″ to 2″ tail, run it in and out of the backing, and later clip the short end that's left at the back. An alternative when starting is to stitch over the tail as you work.

The following stitches are particularly attractive for rugs. Still others can be used, of course, as well as variations on those given. Instructions are for canvas mesh, 4 holes per inch; adjust stitch size to the backing you are using.

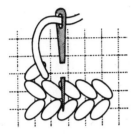

KNITTING OR SOUMAK STITCH

A diagonal stitch with a herringbone effect. Bring needle back to front, *insert front to back 1st hole above and to the right (or left, according to direction of line being worked). Emerge through hole directly below. Repeat from*. For herringbone, move left in next row. Stitch can be made larger by being worked over more threads.

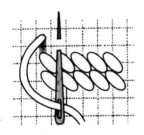

HALF CROSS OR TENT STITCH

A diagonal stitch. Insert needle front to back (tail is on top). *Bring needle through hole directly above. Insert front to back one row right of previous stitch. Repeat from*. Left point of stitch is in same hole as right point of stitch of neighboring row.

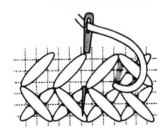

CROSS STITCH

A square stitch composed of two diagonals crossing in the center. Understitch acts as padding for upperstitch. Do all stitches in one direction, then cross them on return journey. Bring needle back to front, insert diagonally at upper right, and emerge at lower right. Continue for row. At row end, emerge at lower right, cross over the understitch, and insert front to back at upper left. Emerge lower right. Continue for row.

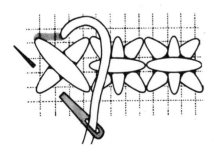

DOUBLE CROSS OR SMYRNA STITCH

A combination stitch: a straight cross over a cross stitch, worked in a square that has an uneven number of holes. Start bottom left. *Bring needle back to front, insert diagonally at upper right, and emerge upper left. Insert diagonally at lower right, and emerge upper middle. Insert at lower middle and emerge left side middle. Insert at right side middle. This is one stitch. Repeat from*.

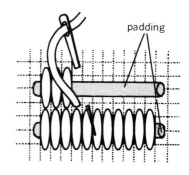

padding

GOBELIN OR TAPESTRY STITCH

Produces a ribbed or corded effect. Start bottom left. Bring needle back to front. Insert 2 holes above. *Emerge at bottom of previous stitch and one hole to right. Insert 2 holes above. Repeat from*. Begin next row in top hole of previous row. Stitch can be worked in parallel lines over 2, 3, or more threads. Stitch shown is being worked over fabric padding. Lay padding on backing and stitch over it.

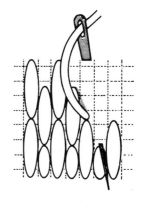

HUNGARIAN STITCH

A vertical stitch in brick formation. Bring needle back to front at lower left. Insert 4 holes up and emerge to right of where 1st stitch began. Insert 2 holes up and emerge at lower right again. Insert 4 holes up. Continue row in this 4–2–4–2 manner. Return to left for next row. Emerge in same space as top of 1st stitch. Insert 4 holes up, emerge in top of 2nd stitch in bottom row. Continue row, moving up 4 for every stitch. Stagger last row in same manner as 1st. Other variations are possible.

RYA OR GHIORDES KNOT

Formed around 2 or more warp ends. Insert needle front to back between 2 ends and emerge left of ends. Insert right of ends and emerge between them. This is one knot. For 2nd knot, if pile gauge is used, place it flat on backing and over the yarn. Make knot, then go under and over gauge to begin 3rd knot. Leave loop loose until stitch is completed, then pull tight (this tends to make gauge stand up). Continue, making subsequent knots around gauge. For looped pile, slide gauge out at end of row; for cut pile, cut yarn at top of gauge. When beginning or ending a length, leave an end equal to pile height. A pile gauge gives an even pile; for uneven pile, wind yarn around hand or fingers, or precut for many color changes.

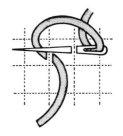

beginning knot

All knots fall in one direction, but once pile is walked on it will spread in all directions. To compensate for directional fall, do the following: when 5 rows are left to do, turn rug around for every 5th knot, or work backwards. In 4th row, work every 4th and 5th knot backwards; in 3rd row, every 3rd, 4th, and 5th knot, and so on until the last row, when all knots are worked backwards, as shown.

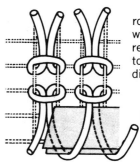

row of knots worked in reverse order to compensate for directional fall

pile gauge

13	14	15	16
9	10	11	12
5	6	7	8
1	2	3	4

Key: Stitch Pattern for Patchwork Sampler

1. Knitting 2 strands beige.

2. Hungarian 3 strands each, dark brown and light olive. First and last rows, 4-2-4-2; all others, 4-4-4-4.

3. Double cross 3 strands each, orange and tan. Work stitch 5 holes square.

4. Gobelin 3 strands each, dark green and dark brown. Work in vertical direction over the following number of threads for each color. A = green, B = brown. 4A, 2B, 2A, 4B, 3A, 2B, 5A, 3B, 2A.

5. Cross 2 strands orange in heavy, braided yarn; 3 brown in different shades. Design is off-center square.

6. Gobelin 2 strands each, off-white and dark gray. Work over 2 threads.

7. Half cross 3 strands each olive and two shades of gold.

8. Cross 2 strands orange in heavy yarn.

9. Hungarian 2 strands gold. Work same as #2.

10. Half cross 2 strands orange, 3 rust.

11. Cross 3 strands gray, 4 green. Work stitch 4 holes square.

12. Double cross 3 strands brown (2 medium, 1 dark). 2 strands tan. Work same as #3.

13. Double cross 3 strands black, 1 gray. Work same as #3.

14. Gobelin 2 strands heather brown. Work in vertical direction over 3 threads.

15. Hungarian 1 strand tan in heavy, braided yarn; 3 rust in fine yarn. Vary stitch: first and last rows, 3-5-3-5; all others, 3-3-3-3.

16. Half cross 2 strands tan in very heavy yarn, 4 gold (2 olive, 2 gold).

Finishing. If your rug is a rya made on Scandinavian backing, you can finish it by hemming or binding (page 28), or you can add a fringe (page 33) or unravel the two cut edges to make a self-fringe (page 34) or a Swedish braid (page 29).

On other backings, hem rug if not done before. If already hemmed, you need only steam press (page 30). Although a lining (page 36) is optional, I strongly recommend it. It will be necessary, of course, if you add an interlining. An interlined flat embroidered rug will last longer and will be more luxuriously soft. Heavy flannel, terry cloth, or any soft double- or single-woven cloth can be used. Pin interlining to backing so that it overlaps hem for ½″ or extends under unmade hem for ½″. Do not turn raw edges of interlining but take close running stitches along them. Tack to backing at various points throughout. Make the hem, if not done before, and stitch to underlining.

patchwork sampler

This sampler will serve to introduce you to the embroidery stitches. It is 16″ square, composed of 16 squares, each 4″ wide and 4″ long. If you adopt this idea for a rug, you can make the squares larger if you wish. For example, enlarge squares to 8″ for a 32″ × 32″ rug, to 10″ for a 40″ × 40″ rug, or to 1′ for a 4′ square rug. Or add squares wherever needed to fit the area planned for the rug. The sampler uses approximately 11 oz. of yarn for a surface coverage of 256″; based on this you can estimate amounts for any rug size.

Arrange to have light, bright, and dark colors scattered throughout rather than grouped together. In the sampler, earth and natural tones are used primarily, with a highlight of various shades of orange.

Size. 16″ × 16″ (working size, 19″ × 19″). The working size allows for a 1½″ hem all around. Allow 2″ for rug hem.

Backing. Canvas mesh, 3½ holes per inch (or other backings).

Material. Rug yarn (light-, medium-, and heavyweight wool and synthetics).

Other. Tapestry needle. Heavy sewing thread for hem. Lining or binding as needed.

Directions. Measure and mark working size on backing. Cut shape out, turn hem, miter corners, and stitch down (see Hemming and Binding, page 28). Mark off 4″ squares with a felt-tipped pen. For this sampler an edging was made using two strands of medium-weight yarn in the blanket stitch (page 58). The braid stitch (page 58) can also be used.

Listed to the left are the stitches used in each square and the yarn amounts in each needleful. Colors are also given, but since this is a patchwork pattern, it is hoped that you will use your own color ideas and make plans according to the yarns on hand. Refer to pages 60–61 for stitch directions. For **Finishing,** see above.

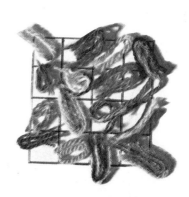

Plan colors for your sampler by arranging snips of yarn in different positions. Shown are colors for sampler below.

A sampler for "Patchwork" rug. Ideal for using up leftover yarn. Sampler incorporates all the stitches (but rya) described on pages 60–61.

inspiration sampler

This design combines four stitches that range from the flat look of the tent and Hungarian stitches to the pile of the rya knot. Colors and types of yarn are given, but you can adapt design to fit your own needs.

Size. Sampler, 13″ × 18″ (working size, 16″ × 21″). This sampler can be enlarged to a 4′4″ × 6′ rug (working size, 4′8″ × 6′4″) by using a grid to transfer the design (page 26). The working sizes allow for a 1½″ hem for sampler and a 2″ hem for rug.

Backing. Canvas mesh, 3½ or 4 holes per inch (or other backing). For sampler, ½ yd., 32″ wide; for rug, 1¾ yds., 79″ wide.

Material. Rug yarn (heavy- and medium-weight wool, medium-weight Persian wool, and rayon).

Other. Tapestry needle. Heavy sewing thread for hem.

Total weight of sampler is approximately 10 oz. Rug weight is about 10 lbs., and is apportioned as follows:

    8 oz. Blue medium-weight hard twist wool for edging stitch.
    6½ lbs. Assorted blues and turquoises of medium- and heavy-weight wool.
    4 oz. Shocking pink rayon (used in stitch C in list on facing page).
    12 oz. 4 oz. each of pink, rose, and orange medium-weight wool.
    1 lb. Red medium-weight wool.
    1 lb. Deep rose medium-weight wool.

Directions. Measure and mark working size on backing. Cut out shape, turn hem, miter corners, and stitch down (see Hemming and Binding, page 28). Transfer pattern using felt-tipped pen. For edges, use heavy rug yarn in a braid stitch (page 58), or, as here, 2 strands medium-weight hard twist rug wool.

The stitches used are listed on the facing page; also, the number of strands that should be in a needleful in order to cover the backing with a stitch of the particular yarn weight used. Do the flat areas first, then proceed to the pile stitches. Refer to pages 60–61 for stitch directions.

Finishing. See page 62. If you line rug, you will need 3½ yds. of 45″ fabric. Since the lining will not be wide enough, seam two pieces together. Binding will use 7 yds.

Detail of embroidered rug, by Zeruah Higley Guernsey Caswell, Vermont, 1832–35. Courtesy of The Metropolitan Museum of Art. Gift of Katharine Keyes, 1938, in memory of her father Homer Eaton Keyes.

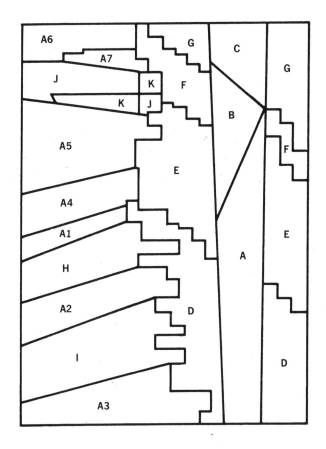

Sketch for "Inspiration" rug can be adapted for a larger rug. The stitches and yarn used in the sampler are keyed to the letters and/or numbers in this diagram.

"Inspiration" sampler. Design was suggested by a calendar photograph of crystals taken through a microscope.

Key: Stitch Pattern for "Inspiration" Sampler

A. Hungarian
 1. 3 strands. Soft medium-weight wool (turquoise).
 2. 3 strands. 2 Persian wool (deep rose), 1 medium-weight (red).
 3. 3 strands. 1 Persian wool (deep rose), 2 medium-weight (red).
 4. 3 strands. Medium-weight wool (1 each: pink, rose, orange).
 5. 1 strand. Heavy 3-ply wool (home-dyed turquoise).
 6. 3 strands. Soft medium-weight wool (2 dull turquoise, 1 greenish turquoise).
 7. 3 strands. Soft medium-weight wool (blue/purple tweed).

B. Half cross 2 strands. Soft heavyweight wool (pale blue).

C. Half cross 3 strands. 2 soft heavyweight wool (pale blue), 1 rayon (shocking pink).

D. Double cross 2 strands. Soft heavyweight wool (pale blue).

E. Double cross 3 strands. Soft medium-weight wool (turquoise).

F. Double cross 2 strands. Hard-twist medium-weight wool (blue).

G. Double cross 2 strands. Soft medium-weight wool (blue/purple tweed).

H. Rya same as A2. Made over a #11 knitting needle. Uncut loop, approximately ½″ high.

I. Rya 2 strands. 1 soft heavyweight wool (pale blue), 1 soft medium-weight wool (turquoise). Same structure as **H.**

K. Rya 2 strands. 1 medium-weight wool (blue), 1 Persian wool (deep rose). Made over pile gauge. 1″ high cut loop.

Repeat design pattern

A   B   C   A

Latch Hook

Since this technique uses precut yarn, you can change yarn and color with every knot and have different pile heights.

Tools. Latch hook (you could try a crochet hook instead, but slightly more skill is needed since there is no latch to hold the yarn in place). Automatic yarn cutter or yarn gauge (page 18).

Backings. Canvas mesh, 3½ to 4 holes per inch. Other stiff, open-spaced backings can be considered (see pages 22–23).

Materials. Rug yarn. Fine yarns can be combined with heavy- and medium-weight ones. Cut your own or purchase precut in 1-oz. packages. Fabric strips—knits or tight weaves—can be tried.

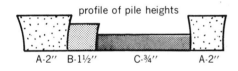

profile of pile heights

A-2″   B-1½″   C-¾″   A-2″

"Sonata"—repeat sampler below for allover design. There are 3 pile heights. **A.** High—3 strands per knot, put in every other row, every hole. Put in every row when used to outline low pile. **B.** Medium—4 strands per knot, put in every row, every hole. **C.** Low—1 strand per knot, put in every row, every hole. Leave untrimmed for uneven pile.

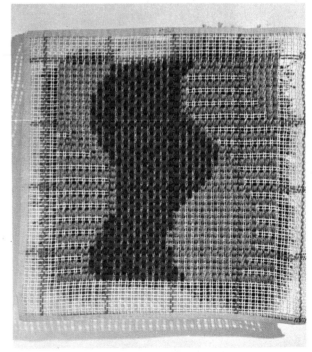

B–4″   C–2½″   A–5″

"Sonata" sampler. Pile strands are shown below sampler in their working lengths.

Back of sampler shows spacing of knots. Masking tape is used on edges instead of overcasting. Remove before hemming.

DESIGN AND DIMENSIONS

Designs for high pile are kept fairly simple and bold, those for 1″ pile can be more involved. The highest pile that still allows for ease of walking is 3″ to 4″, depending on yarn thickness. For further interest, try combining this technique with flat embroidery stitches, or mix two or three colors in one knot. Since the mesh backing lends itself readily to being joined (page 30), it is possible to make a very large rug.

You can use graph paper to transfer a design from sketch to backing, or you can do the rug by counting squares. (This is no problem on the mesh since the holes are so large.) Or you can make a full-scale drawing. See Transferring, page 26.

BEFOREHAND PREPARATIONS

To precut yarn, see page 18. Cut fabrics into strips ¼″ to ½″ wide (page 19). Working length is about twice finished length plus 1″ for the knot. For 2″ pile, cut lengths 4½″ to 5″. Lengths shorter than 2½″ to 3″ (for 1″ pile) are difficult for the hook to handle.

Make a 1½″ to 2″ hem (page 28). The outer rows of knots are made through the hem fold, supplying extra strength to the edges. If you can increase the amount of yarn in these areas still more protection will be provided. If you plan a fringe, leave one row of empty spaces on the sides.

TECHNIQUE

A latch-hooked rug is simply made, although it takes a little time to build up rhythm and gain speed. Work with the mesh lying flat on a table. When you are more adept, you can fold it to align the row you are working on with the table edge, or you can hold the canvas in your lap. Arrange the yarn around you so it is easy to pick up for each knot. Also, have the design sketch handy for referral.

To make the knot, see diagram. Start at the bottom and work horizontally row by row. You can also work in blocks, but do not jump around the pattern until you are more practiced in the technique and in counting the squares of the design. If the yarn resists being pulled through the mesh it is a sign that the yarn is too heavy or that too many strands are being used. Allow one or two empty holes between rows of 2″ to 2½″ pile. An alternative is to stagger the rows—that is, in one row make a knot in every even-numbered hole, in the next row make a knot in every odd-numbered hole, and then continue to alternate. The knots will stand up to give a tight pile and one that will not fall in any specific direction. To even off a short pile, shake the rug or brush it with a stiff brush, then trim all the long ends that are brought up this way.

Finishing. A lining (page 36) is optional, but it gives the rug a more finished look and protects it against wear. If a lining is not used, sew rug binding over the hem (pages 28–29). A fringe may also be added (page 33).

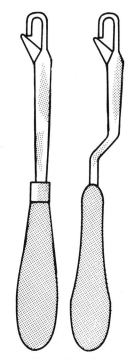

Two models of latch hooks. Next to hook is latch, a hinged piece of metal that opens and closes in use.

How to use latch hook

 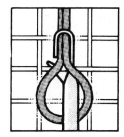

1. Double yarn around shaft, pass hook through holes until open latch clears thread.

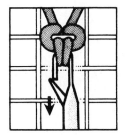 

2. Bring yarn up, around, and under hook. Pull down to close latch. Tug knot to make firm.

FOUR VARIATIONS FOR FLORAL MOTIF REPEAT

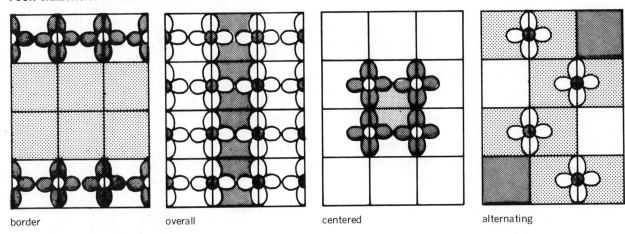

border   overall   centered   alternating

repeat floral design

The two halves of the floral design can be repeated for a rug, as in the examples above, or in any manner you select. Although the lines seem definite in the sketch, they are not so in the rug, since the long pile falls over and presents constantly changing outlines to each flower. Basically, there are two colors, a deep and a light hue, but within these, many close hues and values are mixed so that the main colors appear richer and more intense.

Size. Sampler, 14″ × 14″ (working size 17″ × 17″); full rug, 42″ × 56″ (working size 46″ × 60″). Working size allows a 1½″ hem for sampler and a 2″ hem for rug. The squares can be made larger, or they can be varied in size if you do not plan an overall repeat. If the rug is not too cumbersome, work it as a unit rather than in sections (there will be less waste of backing).

Backing. Canvas mesh 3½ to 4 holes per inch. For sampler, ½ yd., 32″ wide; for rug, 1½ yds., 79″ wide.

Materials. Rug yarn (light- and medium-weight wool, Scandinavian rya, Persian, and polyester) and knitting worsted. Lining (optional): 1¾ yds., 45″ wide for rug. Or 5½ yds. of rug binding. Cut yarn into 5″ to 6″ lengths. A 14″ square uses about 13 oz. of yarn; a 42″ × 56″ rug, about 10 lbs. Of sampler yarn, two-thirds was for background color and one third for floral motif. For center color, about 1 oz. was used for sampler and 10 to 11 oz. for rug. If a pattern other than an overall repeat is used, estimate color proportions according to the number of solid color and patterned squares.

Directions. Measure and cut working size out of backing. Make hem and miter corners (page 28). Transfer pattern to graph as shown at left. Begin first knot in lower left corner and work across row.

Finishing. Either line rug (page 36) or attach binding (pages 28–29).

Graph for floral motif

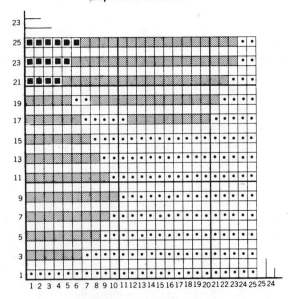

Graph for floral motif **A** at lower left section of repeat (see facing page). Shown is ¼ of pattern; it corresponds to canvas mesh 4 holes per inch (3½ holes per inch can be used for larger squares). Follow numbers to continue design. Symbols refer to color changes. Put stitches in numbered rows.

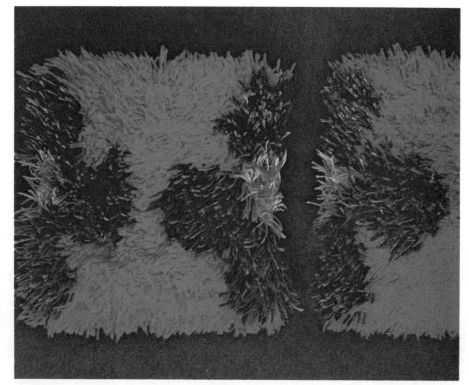

Sketch for floral motif

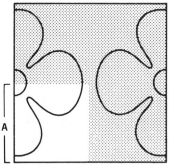

Floral sampler. The whole flower comes into being when two completed sections are joined.

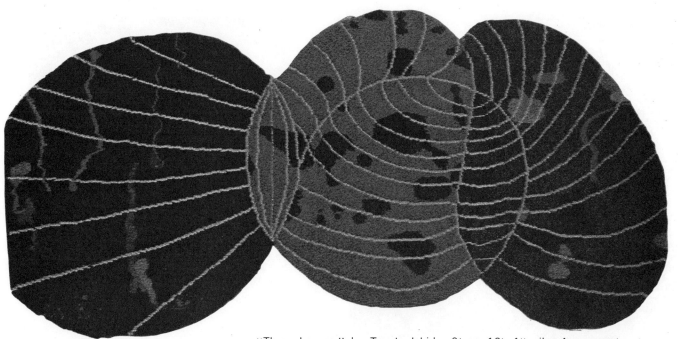

"Three Leaves," by Traute Ishida. 9' × 12'. 1" pile. An example of creating a latch-hook rug of unique design.

Sample for knitted or crocheted rug. Parts of selected block can be embellished with other techniques to add texture and decoration.

CHECKERBOARD RUG
with embroidery chain stitch

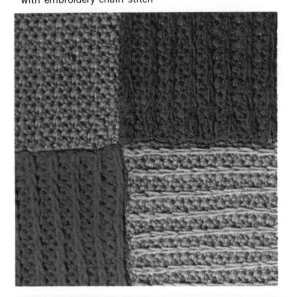

CHECKERBOARD RUG
with rya knots

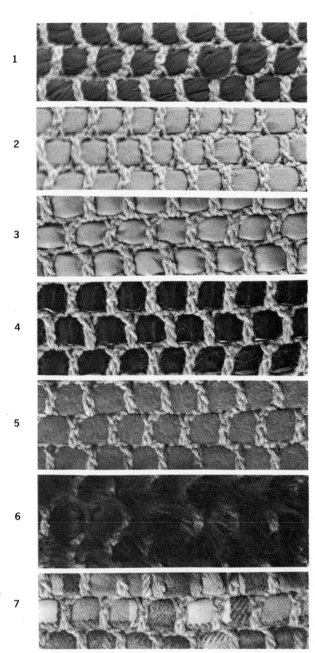

Different materials can be interwoven through crochet base—7 possibilities are shown here. Two or more can be combined in one rug.

CROCHET FILET MESH

1 Nylon stockings (dyed)
2 Felt
3 Leather
4 Vinyl
5 Terry cloth
6 Fur
7 Wool fabric

Crocheting and Knitting

The two techniques are combined here since they are able to share design ideas. The varied texture in each is obtained by the manner in which loops are picked up and drawn through loops already made.

Tools. Crochet hook—large size, I, J, or K. Available in steel (smallest), aluminum (lightest), plastic, and composition bone. Knitting needles—large size, #7, #8, #9. Available in aluminum, plastic, and steel. Extra-large sizes come in wood for both techniques.

Materials. Rug yarn (heavyweight wool, cotton, rayon and cotton, or jute), wool or cotton roving, or synthetics. Knitting worsted or medium-weight rug yarn can be used if doubled for extra thickness. Also rags, stockings, and fabric strips (jersey and other knits are best).

DESIGN AND DIMENSIONS

Texture is in the structure of the stitches. Further texture can be obtained by combining either yarns or fabrics or by adding embroidery stitches onto areas of simple stitches. Pictorial patterns are also possible. Solid color blocks, long strips, squares, and border designs are easy to plan and do. Just draw their sizes and the color placement of the design on wrapping paper. Or areas equal to the size you will be working can be cut out and taped together. Rugs can be room size; work proceeds quickly and sections can be easily joined. Shapes can be of any geometrical variation.

BEFOREHAND PREPARATIONS

Wind yarn into a ball. Cut fabric into strips ¼″ to ½″ wide; if different weights, cut thinner ones wider, thicker ones narrower. Bias-cut strips are favored because of their elasticity and because they do not fray easily, but straight strips can be prepared quicker by tearing instead of cutting. You may fold so that raw edges almost meet at the center, then bring folds together and press (strips can be approximately ¼″ wide when folded), or you may use strips as they are. Frayed threads will soon wear off when the rug is in use, and the stitch is such that further fraying is prevented.

TECHNIQUE

Work a 3″ or 4″ square to find the gauge (page 73). If there are more stitches to the inch than wanted, use a larger hook or needle; if fewer, use a smaller one. The chain stitch in crochet and the cast-on stitches in knitting form the base for the other stitches and set the width of the rug. Work as uniformly as possible so a close construction is maintained; this is important for a firm, durable rug. An open construction is desirable only for a mesh base.

Finishing. If rug is in sections, join on wrong side with a lacing stitch (page 32). Block (page 30) either in sections or after joining. A knitted or crocheted rug is usually not lined, but you may want to strengthen it or add extra thickness (page 36). Rug binding may be used to protect edges or help maintain shape (pages 28–29).

Checkerboard rug pattern

Color key: 9″ squares

—16 squares

—8 squares

—8 squares

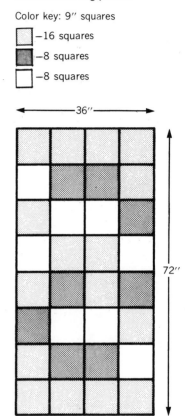

Suggested pattern for filet mesh rug

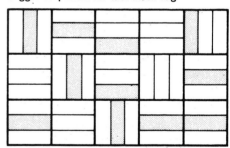

Filet mesh sections joined horizontally or vertically. Vary further by placement of material. Filet can also be crocheted in various colors.

CROCHET STITCHES

The stitches given here are the ones most adaptable for rug use. Hold hook in right hand like a pencil. Hold yarn in left hand, running it between fourth and little finger and over forefinger to give it tension. Do not hold yarn so tightly that it does not move with ease. When making a stitch, insert hook under the *two top loops* of stitch in previous row (see single crochet diagram). Turn work at the end of every row. To finish, pull yarn through last loop to lock stitch. With a needle, run yarn under last two stitches, and trim.

Crochet Abbreviations:

ch—chain
dc—double crochet
sc—single crochet
sk—skip
st(s)—stitch(es)
YO—yarn over needle

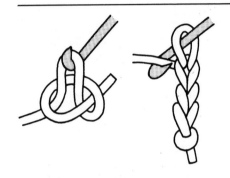

CHAIN STITCH

Make a slip knot near yarn end, leaving a short tail. Insert hook through knot loop and under main length of yarn, then draw a loop through, making first chain stitch. Continue for desired length.

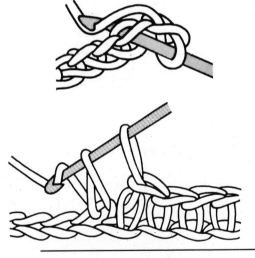

SINGLE CROCHET VARIATION

(To do single crochet, insert hook in ch, YO, draw yarn through. 2 loops are now on hook. YO, draw yarn through both loops.) *To do sc variation:* ch an even number of sts. Row 1: sc in 2nd ch from hook * ch 1, sk 1 ch, sc in next ch. Repeat from * to end of row, ch 1, turn work. For succeeding rows: sc in 1st st * ch 1, sk 1 ch, sc in next st. Repeat from * to end of row, ch 1, turn work.

OPEN OR FILET MESH

Ch for desired length. Double crochet in 6th ch from hook *(to do dc:* YO, insert hook in ch, YO, draw yarn through. 3 loops are now on hook. YO, draw yarn through 2 loops. 2 loops are now on hook. YO, draw yarn through both loops) * ch 2, sk 2 ch, dc in next ch. Repeat from * to end of row, ch 5, turn work. For succeeding rows: dc in dc * ch 2, dc in dc. Repeat from * to end of row, ch 5, turn.

filet mesh rug (pages 70 and 71)

A simple and fast way to produce rugs of countless variations.

Size. Suggested rug, 26″ × 39″, composed of 6 blocks (2 across, 3 down). Each block is 13″ × 13″ after blocking, 12″ × 11″ before.

Materials. Mesh base: heavyweight wool rug yarn, 3½ oz. for one block; 21 oz. for rug. Filler strips: as a guideline, estimate ¾ yds. of 36″ wide material for each 13″ square if strips are cut 3½″ wide. Possibilities for filler are cloth (medium-heavy to heavyweight sportwear, suiting, or coating fabric), felt, terry cloth, stockings or pantyhose, leather, vinyl (leftover scraps, an old raincoat or tablecloth), and fur (an old fur collar or coat: hunt for these in remnant stores—fake is fine).

Tools. Aluminum crochet hook K. Carpet thread or yarn for joining.

Directions. Gauge 2½ sts = 1″. Ch 40 loosely for one block. If rug is to be made in one piece, ch 80. Work base in the filet mesh stitch (facing page). Leave a 2″ to 3″ tail at finish. Pull it through last loop, run into body of square and trim. Completed square should be 14 rows long with 16 filet spaces in each row.

Blocking sets the size and opens the filet spaces; the filler strips hold the size firm. If inserting the strips makes the square longer, either cut strips narrower or undo the number of rows necessary to return to a square shape. If shape is unimportant, and you are making the rug according to the amount of scraps available, but are unable to estimate that amount, do not lock the last stitch. Crochet to the approximate size, then block the piece, and insert the strips. The unlocked stitch will enable you to crochet further if you need more filet or to undo what you have done if you need less.

Filler strips should be as long as the square, plus 2½″ on each end for hemming or for joining to another strip, or they can be sewn on the bias into continuous lengths (page 20). Cut strips 3½″ wide, fold edges to almost meet at center, then bring folds together. Fold does not have to be sewn since it will be held down by the mesh, but you can secure it with safety pins if this makes for easier insertion. Once in, strip will settle to a ⅞″ to 1″ width. Strips can be cut narrower or wider depending on fabric thickness.

As you insert, work fold down with fingers so that it is more to the back of the rug and is invisible from the front. Face all folds in one direction. Weave strip under and over each crochet bar to form an alternate pattern. Keep width tension loose and even so rug does not narrow. If rug is being made in one piece, fold back hem strip allowance so that it is flush with filet border and hem down. If strip is bulky, taper before folding. An optional row of single crochet can be worked around the rug edge as a finishing touch.

Terry cloth frays when cut, but should not fray further if raw edges are properly hidden. Cut off heavy parts of pantyhose or stockings. Use two or more hose as one strand, twist together to insert, and

Embroidery chain stitch. Secure by pulling yarn through 2 edge rug loops. Pick up 2 or 3 rug loops and pull needle through. Tighten chain loop. Repeat.

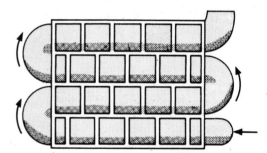

Strips can travel from one row to another. Leaving a large loop will form a scalloped edge.

Gauge is number of stitches in 1″. Garter stitch is shown.

Knitting Abbreviations:

K—knit
P—purl
st(s)—stitch(es)
sl(slip)—pass st from left to right needle without knitting it

Knitting Stitches

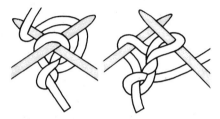

Casting on. Make slip knot, place loop on left needle. Insert right needle, as shown, and draw through to form loop. Insert left needle into st, and sl st. Repeat.

Knit. Keep yarn to back. Insert right needle into 1st st, right to left, as shown, and draw through new loop. Slip old loop off. Repeat until all sts are on right needle.

Garter stitch. Do knit stitch throughout.

Purl. Keep yarn to front. Same as knit, except right needle enters st left to right.

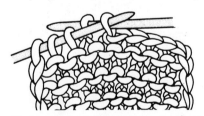

Binding off (at finish). K 2 sts, * pass 2nd st over 1st and off needle, knit another st and repeat from * until 1 st remains. Cut yarn, draw tail through last st and interweave to secure.

spread out to fill space. To join, overlap and sew with same color thread. Stagger so all joinings do not fall together. If heavy leather is used, fold to a width of 1″. If strip unfolds while being interwoven, secure with a few drops of glue or rubber cement. Stiff leather can be trimmed to a straight decorative edge that will extend ½″ to ¾″ beyond crochet edge. Instead of sewing, use glue for leather or for vinyl. A lightweight vinyl works best in the rug. Different furs can be used in one rug. Cut on skin side with a sharp razor blade. A long-haired fur rolls over on itself so that raw edges are concealed. Do not overlap when joining; instead, place strips side by side and sew together with a lacing stitch (page 32). After insertion, pull up fur that is held down by crochet bar so that as much as possible is on the surface.

Finishing. Put sections on floor in desired positions and join together (page 30).

checkerboard rug (pages 70–71)

This rug can be knitted or crocheted; its design is based on the rug being made in sections of different colors which are then assembled to form a color pattern. Half a rug can usually be done in a day. You can also embellish the rug with other techniques. An embroidery chain stitch and a rya knot, both of which add texture and weight, are used here. They can be placed in every square or in selected ones. The chain stitch can run horizontally or vertically, with the parallel rows spaced as close together or as far apart as you wish for your particular pattern. The rya knot can be put in with a needle (page 61) or a latch or crochet hook (page 67). Add chain stitch (page 73) before sections are blocked and joined; rya after.

Size. 36″ × 72″, composed of 32 9″ squares (4 across, 8 down). These proportions can be changed to fit the space in your room.

Materials. Wool rug yarn, heavyweight (or two medium weights used as one). Each square, 2-3 oz.; rug, 4 lbs. Embroidery chain stitch: rug yarn, heavy and medium weight, 9 oz. (3 colors, each 3 oz.) if used in every other square. Rya knot: fine and heavy yarns, 32 oz. (2 colors, each 16 oz.) if used in every other square.

Tools. Aluminum crochet hook I. Knitting needle #7.

Directions. Gauge: 3 sts = 1″. For crochet, ch 30, work sc variation for 30 rows, then end off. For knitting, cast on 30, work garter stitch until square measures 9″. When blocking, try not to stretch much beyond that measure. Work tightly.

Suggested for a block: 9 or 10 rows of embroidery stitches. Use yarn to contrast with those in the rug body. Rust, tan, and brown were used for the blocks here (see page 71 for suggested distribution of color). Over the brown is embroidered 3 strands of medium-weight rug yarn in a contrasting brown. Over the tan, 1 strand of heavyweight rug yarn in a contrasting tan; and over the rust, 1 strand of heavyweight rug yarn in an orange-red.

For rya, space the knots and tie them around yarns in the rug body so that two rows of 19 knots each are along the borders (see page 70). Each knot uses 2 strands of yarn. The small center square is 4 knots square. To find center, run two pieces of string diagonally from corner to corner; they will cross at the centerpoint. From there count 2 stitches down and 2 to the left to begin square.

Finishing. Assemble the squares in the color positions you want and join (page 30).

cross-over stitch sampler

Gauge is approximately 3½ sts = 1″. Cast on stitches according to size desired, but you *must* cast on an *even* number. Polyester yarn in various thicknesses from medium weight to heavyweight (soft). Four yarns used as one. Knitting needle #8.

Row 1: *insert needle in front of 1st st, pull 2nd st through 1st, K 2nd st, and slip st off needle. Insert needle in back of 1st st, K 1st st, and slip st off needle. Repeat from * across row. **Row 2:** Purl. **Row 3:** K 1. Repeat **Row 1,** ending K 1. **Row 4:** Purl. Repeat the four rows for pattern.

Four yarns—blue, turquoise, fuschia, and black—used as one in a cross-over stitch in sampler by Dorothy Liebes Design, Inc. Fewer yarns can be combined or yarn used singly. Directions for sampler are given above.

Designs for crocheted and knitted rugs

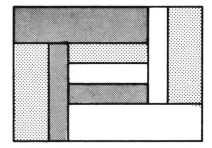

sections of 2 widths in various colors

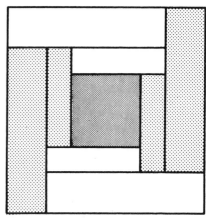

sections of 3 widths in various colors

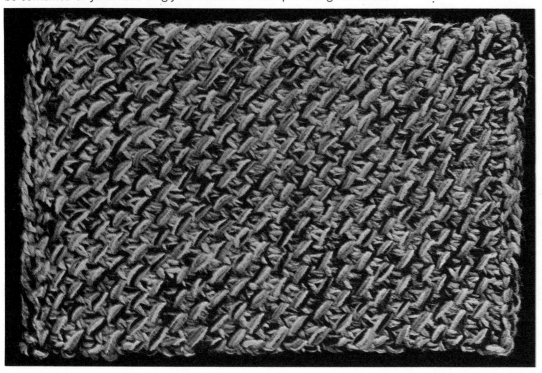

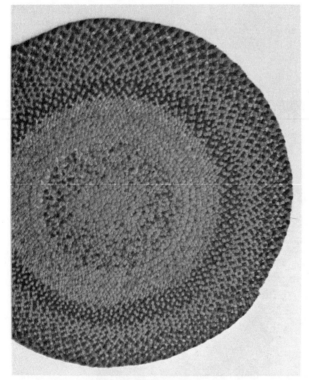

(Above) Rectangular braided rug. Designs are formed in the braiding. (Below) Individual braids laced together and fringed at both ends. Both rugs by Gloria W. Scannell.

(Above) Round braided rug by Shirley Sayles. A dominant color gives rug a contemporary look. Peppered effect was achieved by overdyeing patterned material.

Braiding

A braided rug is solid and sturdy, and has a warm, informal character. Its beauty is in the way colors, solid and patterned, fall against one another in the braid.

Tools. Fabric strip cutter (page 20), or cut or tear by hand. Rug lacer. Long blunt needle. Lacing cord. Clamp. Braid-aids (metal, cone-shaped) are optional but eliminate a lot of work.

Materials. Sturdy woolen fabric. Used fabrics are excellent (page 17). Heavyweight wool rug yarn can be used, as can stockings, cotton, very heavy cord or string, jute (outdoor use), grasses, and raffia.

DESIGN AND DIMENSIONS

One realization you will soon come to in this craft is that even though colors may seem incompatible side by side, they can blend together beautifully once they are braided. You can plan your colors or you can make a hit-or-miss rug by choosing strips at random. One plan might consist of a band of several rows in a color contrasting to the next several rows; more planning results in a graded effect going from light in the center of the rug to dark towards the borders, then lighter. You can stop at any point and consider whether to drop or add certain colors or to repeat or reverse the present color. Designs are also possible; for example, a small arrowhead can be formed by combining two dominant colors with a neutral one. Braided units can be attached to make rugs of various shapes. For a raised pile in some areas, combine braiding with hooking or with the rya knot (see page 61).

BEFOREHAND PREPARATIONS

To prepare fabric, see page 18. Cut or tear (page 19) into widths from 1¼″ for medium- to heavyweight fabric, to 3″ for lightweight fabric. These widths make braids ⅝″ to 1½″ wide. Braids can be as narrow as ½″. Keep in mind that wide braids flatten out faster then narrow ones and do not wear as well. Don't cut all the strips at one time since you may need different widths or want different colors.

Sew the strips together on the bias (right) by hand or machine. Then fold raw edges toward center, bring folds together, and press or baste. You can also fold as you braid by tucking raw edges in with thumb and forefinger; this requires practice, however. Or use braid-aids, which automatically turn raw edges in and fold the fabric as it is being braided (top right). Wind fabric into a flat roll, keeping all seams to the underside, and secure with a blanket pin or by running string through center and tying it. Unwind the roll as you braid and add lengths when needed.

Ideally, all the strips in one rug should be the same weight and width. If you use a variety of fabrics, fold to equal widths, but try not to use too indiscriminate a variety since the wear will be un-

A sampler in position for braiding. Braiding equipment includes lacing cord, rug lacer, and braid-aids. Pattern is hit-or-miss. One color (red) is dominant throughout and is of medium-weight wool, 1¼″ wide. Plaid and tweed strips, which can vary throughout, are of lightweight wool, 1½″ wide. Sampler can be developed into small round rug.

To prepare fabric strips

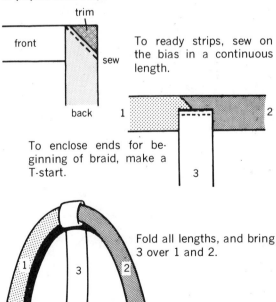

To ready strips, sew on the bias in a continuous length.

To enclose ends for beginning of braid, make a T-start.

Fold all lengths, and bring 3 over 1 and 2.

To start braid

3-strand
Braid left over center,
right over center.

4-strand
Braid 1 over 2, under
3, over 4. Repeat.

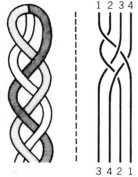

3-strand braid 4-strand braid

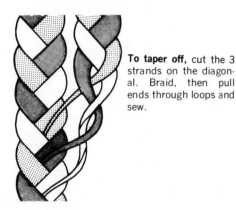

To lace braid to rug, draw cord side to
side through loops.

To taper off, cut the 3
strands on the diagonal. Braid, then pull
ends through loops and
sew.

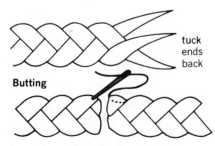

Butting

tuck
ends
back

To prepare for butting, tuck tapered ends
under braided loops, trim, and sew down.
Stitch through loops from one end to the
other so that ends are completely joined.

even. If braid-aids are used, they will automatically fold the fabric
to even widths. Lightweight fabric can be padded with fillers (narrow fabric strips) concealed in the folds.

TECHNIQUE

Pin, sew, or tie the ends of three lengths together, or make a T
start (page 77). If you are using braid-aids, slip them on before enclosing ends. Clamp lengths to a tabletop or tie strong cord around
them and attach to chair back or hook. To make a 3-stranded braid,
see top left. Give each strand a slight tug after each braiding motion
to maintain firm and even tension. Folds can be kept to left or
right, and should not show on the top or bottom of the rug. If kept
to right, they will face the inside of the rug; it is easier to use
braid-aids when folds are kept in that direction. Braids of 4 or 5
strands can also be made, and if strips are thin enough, so can
braids of 6, 7, or more strands.

Round rug. In order for a round rug to lie flat, begin braiding by
bringing left strand over center one, left over center again, and
pull right strand over center tightly. If braids were numbered, the
sequence would be 1 over 2, 2 over 1, and 3 over 2 tightly. Repeat
until circle is about 3″ in diameter. Then start regular braiding.

Oval rug. See diagram, facing page, to determine length of center
braid. Braid the required length; then, to keep the center flat, make
a round turning (facing page). Braid to the beginning of the first
length and lace together. Begin regular braiding.

Square-cornered rug. Braid to desired length for center, then make
two sharp corners (diagram, facing page). Continue regular braiding
to beginning of first length, then sew and lace together. Make third
square corner, braid one or two loops, and make fourth square corner.
Continue in this fashion, making corner turnings whenever necessary.

Lacing. After a reasonable amount has been braided, secure braid
with a clothespin and turn rug over to lace. Work on a flat surface
with the body of the rug away from you. At the start of the rug,
lacing is preceded by sewing. Use a sturdy needle and heavy carpet
thread. Tie a knot, insert needle into first loop, and hide knot in
folds. Sew through the beginning loops to gather them together
(facing page, top). Then remove needle and attach about a yard
of lacing cord to the thread with a square knot. Replace needle
with lacer or blunt needle.

In lacing, the cord is drawn between the loops (left); it does not
penetrate material. Pull cord tight so that loops lock into each other
and cord disappears between them. If cord shows, try to push it
into folds; if it still shows, skip a loop on braid being attached.
Ease in fullness on curves by skipping alternate loops on the braid
being attached. When a length of cord is about to end, tie another
to it with a square knot. Cloth strips can be used in place of cord.
When you change color, mark the place with a safety pin and make
future changes in the same area. On an oval rug, change on a curve.

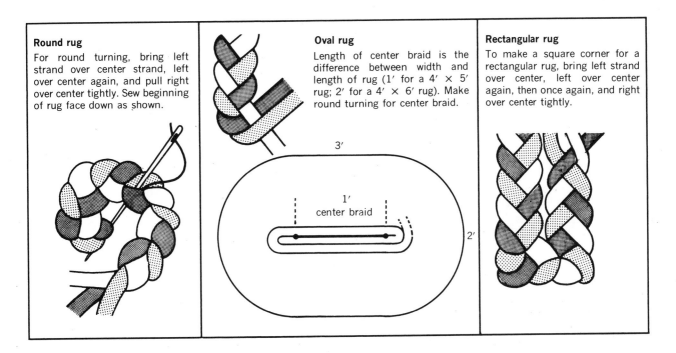

Round rug

For round turning, bring left strand over center strand, left over center again, and pull right over center tightly. Sew beginning of rug face down as shown.

Oval rug

Length of center braid is the difference between width and length of rug (1′ for a 4′ × 5′ rug; 2′ for a 4′ × 6′ rug). Make round turning for center braid.

3′

1′
center braid

2′

Rectangular rug

To make a square corner for a rectangular rug, bring left strand over center, left over center again, then once again, and right over center tightly.

Tapering. To finish the rug, remove braid-aids and cut strips, leaving 6″ or more to end off with. (The length left will depend on the size of the rug.) Taper each end (facing page) so that its width gradually decreases to a long tapering point. On an oval rug, taper off on a curve. On a rectangular rug, taper for only a couple of inches. Replace braid-aids and continue braiding.

When strips become too thin to be held by braid-aids, fold in raw edges and sew folds together. Braid and lace, then insert ends into the rug (facing page). Secure them with invisible stitches.

Butting. Although this may be a bit advanced for a beginner, it is included since it allows for distinct color changes and gives a more finished ending to the rug. Butted rounds are individual braids added on one at a time. If you wish to butt, start the rug in a continuous braid as usual, then taper off and butt the rest, or make the rug as large as you wish and then begin butting where you want a solid band of color, or just butt the last few rows.

To butt, first taper off the rug. Then take three new strands (do not enclose ends) and braid a length long enough to go around the rug. Lace this round to the rug starting a little beyond the tapered off point and ending almost where the two ends of the round meet. Braid a little beyond that point, then taper strands at both ends and tuck them under the last loops. Tweezers or pliers will help here.

Trim any protruding ends and stitch them down. Butt the two ends of the round head on (see diagram at bottom of facing page) and stitch through the loops from one end to the other until secured. Then finish lacing.

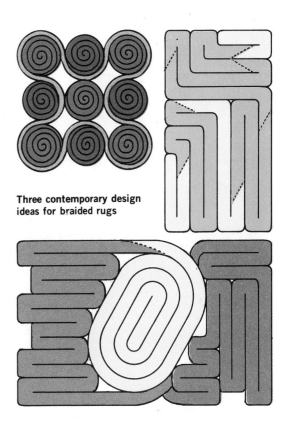

Three contemporary design ideas for braided rugs

Hooking

Hooking allows the greatest design freedom; it ranges from the most intricate detailing to surface patterns caused by the direction of the loops. High and low pile and cut and uncut loops are additional design possibilities.

Tools. Hand hook (hooked metal shank fitted in wooden handle—or try a #1 or #2 steel crochet hook), punch needle (metal needle in wooden handle), speed hooks (such as the shuttle hook or egg-beater), or electric needle (a drill-like tool). Frame (see page 24): optional for hand hook; essential for others. Fabric strip cutter (page 20), or cut by hand. Scissors (bent-handled ones preferred for cutting loops).

Backings. Choose one that is strong, loosely woven, and easy to hook through (see pages 22–23).

Materials. All sorts of fabrics, new or used (page 17). Also string, leather, ribbon, or just about any yarn (but be wary of uneven textures as they may not go through the speed hooks).

DESIGN AND DIMENSIONS

All manner of pictorial and geometric designs are possible. You actually draw with the hook, emphasizing a shape or a line by the direction of the hooking. Colors can be blended to create texture or to effect subtle shading. Rug shape ranges from simple rectangles, circles, ovals, and half-circles to curves and free forms. Size is no problem since backing is easily joined. Yarn and fabric can be mixed, as can looped and cut pile. Pile heights, depending on the tool, can range from ¼″ to 3″. Combine fine strips with heavy ones, and use different widths to outline a single row or to provide pleasant textural contrast.

Pattern and background can be hooked in straight rows, in lines of various angles, or in those contoured to the design. Define design shapes by outlining them in the same color as the design or in background colors. Or omit outlines to obtain a soft, indefinite pattern. In hooking, any mistakes or changes of heart about color or design are no great tragedy—just pull out the area and rehook it.

Use a grid to transfer pattern to backing. Make reverse tracings for punch needle and speed hooks. (See Transferring, pages 26–27.)

BEFOREHAND PREPARATIONS

Any length strip can be used for the hand hook. Short lengths are not used for punch needle or speed hooks; a beginner can start by using 1½ to 2 yd. lengths. To prepare material, see page 18. Average fabric widths are 3/32″ to ¼″. Cut backing, allowing at least 2″ for the hem. Overcast edges with cotton thread, then transfer pattern. Center backing and attach backing to frame with staple gun, tacks, or laces. Use enough to insure tautness. For extra strength, double backing where it will be attached. For backings larger than

"Blue Prayer Rug," by Eleanor Smoler. 24½″ × 61″. Design inspired by antique Oriental rug.

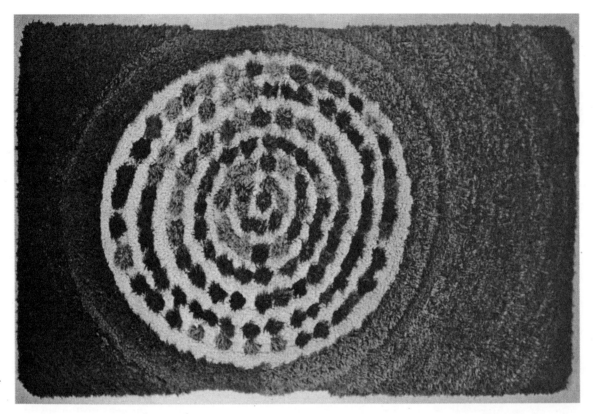

"Circuit," by Marla Mallett. 42″ × 64″. Multi-level pile heights contribute to overall effect.

Sample rug, by Dorothy Liebes Design, Inc. 18″ × 24″. Inspired by peasant folk art.

frame size, fold the excess and attach through it. On a rectangular roller frame, the excess is taken up by the roller. For a hoop frame, put backing over bottom hoop, fit top hoop over both, and adjust tension. There should be enough clearance on all sides of the pattern so that the hook does not come into contact with frame edges. If you are hooking in sections, which will then be joined, allow an area of 1½″ to 2″ for overlapping (page 32).

Since pressure while hooking can cause the backing to stretch slightly, lacing is worth considering as a fairly quick way of tightening it again. Use sturdy twine or cord that can take a lot of tension.

Tie lacing around one corner of the frame, thread it through a rug needle, and begin lacing the backing to the sidebars, pulling as you do so to get maximum tension. Cut and tie lacing at each corner and start anew. The needle should be inserted into the backing about 1″ to 1½″ from the edges and laces spaced about 1″ apart. Lacing can be pulled in at the corners to tighten any sag. If the frame has rollers top and bottom, turn the top roller until backing is very taut and lace as shown on page 82, top. A lacing set with metal hooks and lacing cord can be used for this frame.

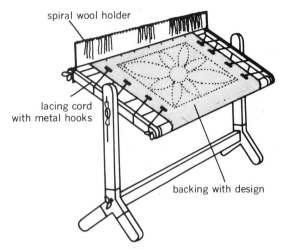

spiral wool holder

lacing cord with metal hooks

backing with design

Set up for hooking on rectangular roller frame. Backing is laced to frame with metal clips and lacing cord. A spiral wool holder is attached at top.

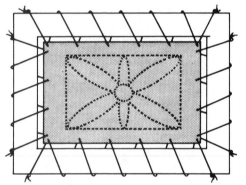

Homemade rectangular frame with backing laced in position.

TECHNIQUE

Do a practice piece before starting the rug, or practice in the background of the rug pattern. Work from right to left. When you want to change direction or travel to another row, cut the strip on the front of the rug and begin anew. Never cross over from one direction to another. The beginning end of the strip should be brought to the front of the work, as should the tail end; both are then clipped to the height of the pile. There should be no ends on the underside of the rug. First practice straight rows (once you are experienced, you can meander all over the backing). At the end of each row, cut the strand and start the next row at the beginning of the first. Vary by doing curved lines and wavy ones, traveling straight across the backing, then diagonally. Play with different shapes to see the effects that are possible.

Try different spacing; if backing can be easily seen between loops, then you must hook closer together. It is important to have the backing firmly packed since this is what holds the stitches in, but do not place the loops so close that the backing buckles. There should be enough room for the loops to unfold. Usually low loops are spaced one or two backing threads apart; high loops, or those using heavy materials, are spaced farther apart. Check the reverse side of the backing for the spacing also. Ideally, the back of the work should look like a series of color dots, but a beginner may not achieve this at first. Try to make loops as nearly the same height as possible; this will be easier to control as you get into the rhythm of the work. But if they are not absolutely even, this imperfection, like home-dyeing, will only add to the charm of the work.

Lines can be curved or colors mixed in one loop for a tweeded effect.

Note color differences between loop and cut pile.

Hook the two outside rows around the border of the rug very closely together so as to form a thick edge. This will protect the edges from heavy wear and prevent any backing from showing through when the hem is turned under.

Each hook requires a slightly different technique. The hand hook can be held at any angle, but the punch needle and speed hooks are worked perpendicular to the backing. With the hand hook, you work with the front of the rug facing you and pull the loops up to the surface; with the others, you work on the reverse side and push the loops through to the front. Punch needle and speed hooks come with complete directions. They adjust to different heights and have interchangeable needles for different width materials. Thread needles and adjust gauges before beginning to work. Only the hand hook and punch needle can accommodate very heavy materials.

Use whichever hook suits you the best. The punch needle and speed hooks are well suited for fast work, but if you are in no great rush to finish your rug, then the hand hook is the perfect tool. It is relaxing to work with and has the advantage of being able to use short leftover ends of material. You can also use more than one hook to make a ring.

Hand hook. Hold the hook in your right hand. If the hook is short enough, you can fit its handle into the palm of your hand and keep your index finger on its shank. Buy a hook that is comfortable for you. Your left hand holds the strip under the backing and feeds it to the hook. Push hook through backing as far as it will go, catch the beginning of the strip and pull it up. Push hook through again and catch strip, giving a slight twist to your wrist as you do so, and pull first loop up. Continue in this fashion (top, right). If you are not using a frame, your left hand holds the backing steady and feeds the yarn as well.

Punch needle. Face the slotted side of the needle in the direction you are going to work and push it through the backing as far as it will go. The needle works best for a beginner when the loop is caught on the underside (the front of the rug) between thumb and index finger and held in place as the needle is pulled out and then pushed in again. Otherwise the loop might pull back with the needle. When the needle is pulled up, bring it just to the surface, and for ease glide it to the left, then plunge it through the backing again. Continue in this fashion (center, right).

Shuttle hook. The hook is held in both hands and is operated by shifting its wooden sections up and down. As the right section is lowered, the needle in it plunges through the backing (bottom, right). As it is raised, the left section lowers to secure the loop. The hook then gives a little jump and skips to the next position, ready to repeat the motion. A nice rhythm can be attained as the sections move up and down. A certain amount of practice is required to maintain proper spacing. However, once you learn to operate this hook, it will travel very quickly and evenly across the backing.

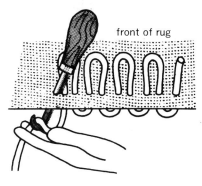

Hand hook method

front of rug

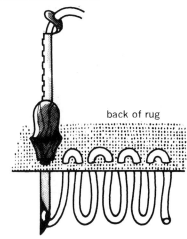

Punch needle method

back of rug

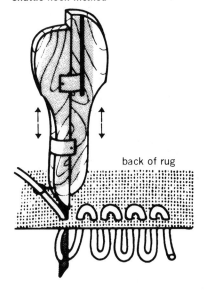

Shuttle hook method

back of rug

Examples of directional hooking.

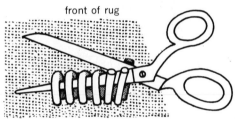

front of rug

To cut pile, fold rug over hand so that loops stand out.

Eggbeater. Use both hands; one to steady and the other to turn the handle that activates the needle.

Electric needle. Easy to operate, but expensive. It is very fast and gives a fairly even pile, but not so even that the rug looks commercially produced. It is possible to get intricate curves with one motion of the needle.

Finishing. If you plan to cut the loops, do so at the finish. You may already have done some in small areas as you were hooking in order to see the color and design effect. Cutting usually deepens or heightens a color that was not very bright to begin with. If you have bent-handled scissors and do not care if a random effect (a mixture of cut and uncut loops) appears, then do the cutting on the frame; otherwise you will find it easier to do when the rug is off the frame (left). Cut any loop that is higher than 1″. Trim to an even pile. If you have made crossovers, cut through them and bring cut ends to the front, or pull them out and rework the area.

Steam the rug (page 30) so the surface will bloom; do not press. Then turn back hem or use rug binding (page 28). The rug can also be lined (page 36) or have latex put on (page 37). Or latex, press hem down, and put on a burlap lining at the same time. Press lining and hem to the underside of the rug so that the latex bleeds through, making the rug skidproof.

Two Rug Designs

butterfly rug design (facing page)

This pattern is for a full-sized rug with rounded corners. Transfer design by dividing it into quarters as shown and faithfully copying the pattern lines from each quarter to corresponding quarter of the backing. Recommended backing size is about 3′ × 4½′. Allow for a 2″ hem. For this size backing, and for a pile of 1″, about 7½ lbs. of wool yarn or fabric strips will be needed: 3 lbs. of color #1, 2 lbs. of color #3, and 1¼ lbs. each of colors #2 and #4. The rug may also be made in a lower pile, or in two pile heights—with the butterfly in relief in a higher pile than the background. Adjust yarn amounts accordingly. The butterfly may also have a multi-color effect, with each area in a different color, shaded from light at outer edges to dark at the center. Two suggestions for color variations are at the top of the facing page.

"BUTTERFLY" RUG DESIGN

Suggested color schemes

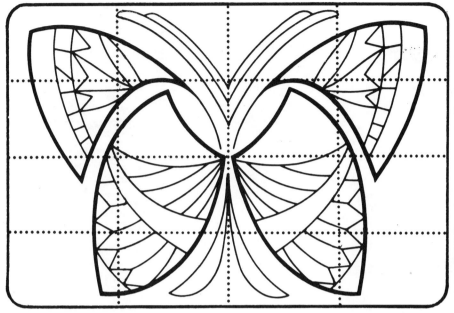

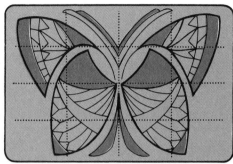

arches

The sampler shown is presented as an exercise in manipulating curves; it can be repeated for a full-sized rug. First outline the contours of the design, then fill in the areas following the direction of the arrows. For a second repeat of the design, you can reverse direction. The sampler is 12″ square and requires about 7 oz. of wool yarn. Pile can be cut or left looped. Yarn amounts and pile heights are: 3 oz. of color A in a ¼″ pile, 1 oz. of color B in a ¾″ pile, and 1½ oz. each of colors C and D in a 1″ or 1¼″ pile. Two colors can be used in an area for a tweeded effect, or areas can be shaded from dark to light, from one edge to the other.

Repeat design pattern

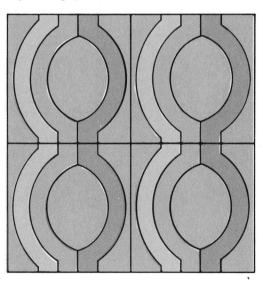

Pile heights:
A—¼″ cut or uncut
B—¾″ cut or uncut
C—1¼″ cut or uncut
D—1¼″ cut or uncut

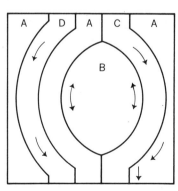

(Above) Rug being woven on harness loom from a sketch. Photo by Glenn Winchester.

(Right) "Icarus," by Nell Znami-erowski. 44" × 80". Collection of "Objects, U.S.A.," The Johnson Collection of Contemporary Crafts. Courtesy of Lee Nordness Galleries, Inc.

Weaving

A woven rug is made up of warp (vertical threads or *ends)* and filling (horizontal threads or *picks).* A beginner using simple equipment and following the techniques here can make different types of woven rugs.

Tools. Frame loom, or an upright carpet or tapestry loom. Shed sticks, stick shuttle, and beater. Pile gauge, for knotted pile (see page 18).

To make a small *frame loom* (right) for rug sections, or a large frame loom for sections or for a small rug, see Lap Frame and Large Frame, page 24.

The *shed sticks* are inserted into the warp. When placed on edge they raise alternate warp ends and make an opening, or shed, for the filling to pass through. When placed flat, they are used to beat down the filling at the start of the rug. You will need two sticks. For each, use a strip of wood slightly longer than loom width, about 1½″ wide, and not more than ¼″ thick. Sand until smooth and rounded; also sand one end to a point to make insertion into the warp easier.

The *shuttle* carries the filling through the warp. It is a flat piece of wood, 10″ to 21″ long, 1¼″ to 2½″ wide, and about ¼″ thick. It is available in weaving supply houses, but you can make your own. A homemade *wooden needle* (right), *butterfly* (page 89), or *bodkin* can be used instead of a shuttle for small areas. A bodkin is a broken-off toothbrush handle sanded to a point.

The *beater* (right) is used to beat down the filling once the rug has progressed to the point where shed sticks can no longer do an adequate job. In its place you can use a fork or a broken-in-half sturdy hair comb (use half with widely spaced teeth). However, they are not as comfortable in the hand as the beater, nor do they have the necessary weight.

Materials. Warp yarn. Should be strong, durable, and fairly smooth, and should not fray or have too much give. When it will be visible, as in a rag rug or in a fringe, consider its color and weight. Cotton and linen are the most common, but other natural or synthetic yarns can be used if they have the above qualities. Yarn thickness determines the number of warp ends per inch, or *sett.* The usual sett is 4 to 8 warp ends per inch. The thicker the yarn, the lower the sett. The finer the yarn, the higher the sett. Fine warp yarns can be doubled or tripled to obtain the lower sett. Some easily available warp yarns follow.

Cotton rug warp (8/4). Sett 8 ends. Comes in numerous colors and is soft and highly serviceable, but has little body as compared to other warp yarns. Recommended for beginners and for making sampler warps. *Cotton seine twine or cable cord* (6 ply). Sett 6 or 8. Highly twisted and very strong. Twists vary; don't buy one that is

Frame loom

nails ¼″ apart

Upright rug loom

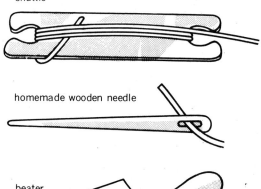

shuttle

homemade wooden needle

beater

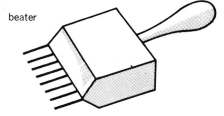

too elastic. *Cotton wrapping twine* (8 to 16 ply). Sett is 8 for fine plies (8 to 10), and 6 or 4 for heavy plies (12 to 16). Both cotton twines are available in pound cones at stationery stores. They come in white only but can be home-dyed if color is needed. *Linen rug warp.* Sett is 4 to 6 for standard yarn. Comes in a natural color that is attractive as a fringe, is stiff and inelastic, and has a firm body. Buy only warp yarn since other linens may fray.

Filling yarn. Use one that is soft but sturdy. Its weight will depend on warp yarn thickness and on the sett. The heavier the warp yarn, or the higher the sett, the finer the filling yarn, and vice versa. Soft yarns compress easily to cover the warp more completely. A flatweave rug requires sturdy yarn since its filling gets direct wear. Rags can also be used for filling.

Pile yarn. Wool has been the preferred choice, but synthetics are being tried more and more. Felt, leather, and bias-cut fabric strips can also be used.

DESIGN AND DIMENSIONS

The rug can be designed to emphasize the beauty and texture of the material used. Both flatweave and pile rugs can be accents of color with simple designs. Using different pile levels, or combining cut and loop pile, or pile with flatweave, will increase design interest. Pile can be as high as 4″. Rugs can be narrow, their sizes limited by the loom, or made of sections joined together for larger sizes. Most rugs are rectangular, but with experimentation it is possible to obtain other shapes. To transfer pattern, see page 26.

BEFOREHAND PREPARATIONS

Establish warp width by marking at the top of the loom where you want the warp to begin and at the bottom where you want it to end. Use tape or pencil. Then estimate the sett. Next, warp the loom—that is, stretch the warp ends in planned order onto the loom (see facing page, top left). Space the ends according to the sett. Reel the warp yarn directly from the cone or spool it is on. Keep tension even but not too taut. If there is a little slack, it will be taken up in the weaving. End where marked by cutting the yarn and tying it around nail. (You might find it easier to warp the loom on its side.) Position shed sticks (facing page, top center). When interweaving them into the warp, consider doubled ends as one.

Prepare filling yarn or rag strips by winding each color or combination of colors onto shuttles or into butterflies.

TECHNIQUE

Follow comprehensive diagram, facing page, for the various techniques. Put a heading in at the start to spread the warp evenly and to provide support during the beating down of the filling. The heading can be of heavy cotton, rags, or cardboard strips, and is removed when rug is finished. Cardboard strips are usually cut ½″ to 2″ wide, but can exceed that when a long fringe is planned (since the fringe is formed by the warp taken up in the heading). If you plan to hem the rug, weave the hem in after the heading.

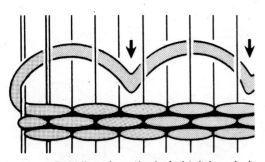

Bubbling. A method of obtaining slack in the filling for better coverage of the warp. Beat down firmly.

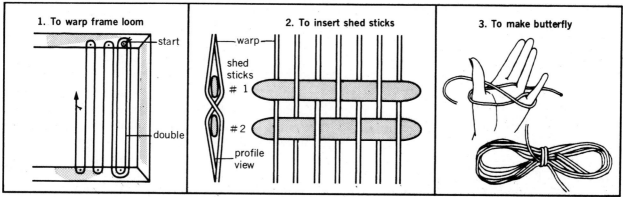

1. To warp frame loom

start

double

2. To insert shed sticks

warp

shed sticks #1

#2

profile view

3. To make butterfly

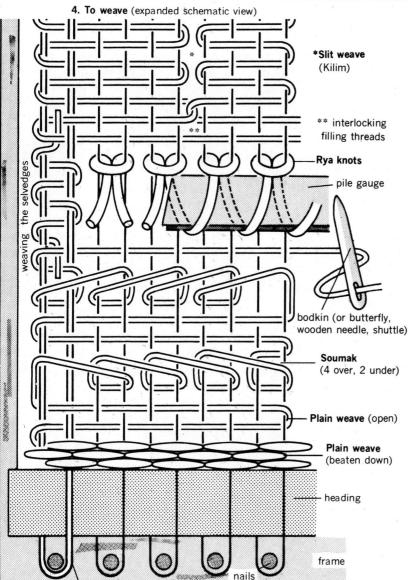

4. To weave (expanded schematic view)

weaving the selvedges

*****Slit weave**
(Kilim)

****** interlocking filling threads

Rya knots

pile gauge

bodkin (or butterfly, wooden needle, shuttle)

Soumak
(4 over, 2 under)

Plain weave (open)

Plain weave
(beaten down)

heading

frame

nails

double warp at each selvedge edge

1. Tie yarn around nail at starting point. Warp as shown. Double ends at both selvedges. Tie around nail at finish.

2. Insert shed stick #1 over-under across width of loom. Push to top. Insert #2 under-over a few inches below. To form opening, or shed, for filling to pass through, turn shed stick on edge.

3. A bundle of yarn used to carry filling through narrow widths, or over pile gauge. To finish, half hitch yarn twice around center.

4. Read sketch from the bottom up
Plain weave. Bring stick #2 a few inches above heading. Open shed. Pass shuttle with filling through from right, leaving a 2″ tail. Close shed and slide stick down to beat 1st pick.

Remove #2 and re-insert at top, under-over from right. Slide #1 down and open shed. Insert shuttle from left, tuck tail around selvedge. Close shed, beat down so no warp is seen. Remove #1 and re-insert from right above #2. Repeat.

Soumak. Count 4 warp ends in and insert yarn front to back between ends 4 and 5. Go back 2 ends, bring yarn **over** surface back to front between ends 2 and 3 (bringing it **under** surface reverses direction). Count 4 warp ends over and repeat.

Rya knots. Close shed and bring yarn up between 2 ends. Yarn on left over-under left end; yarn on right over-under right end. Pull up tight. Continue for row.

Knots are usually not made on selvedges Do plain weave with supplementary yarn, entering the rug body at intervals so selvedges do not become separated from rug.

Slit weave (Kilim). A plain weave that forms slits between areas to allow for color or pattern changes. Use two butterflies, one from each direction. Interlock where yarn meets or leave open. Slits can be sewn together.

Variations in spacing and knot placement

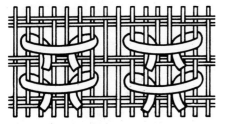

knots spaced apart

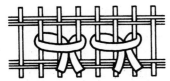

knotting around uneven number

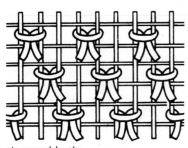

staggered knots

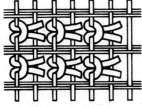

knots formed sideways

Spacing of knots depends on yarn thickness and on the number of warp ends per inch.

Beat heading down tightly but put hem in somewhat looser since it has to be flexible enough to be turned back. Use filling yarn for the hem, but if you find it difficult to cover the warp, since you will be weaving loosely, substitute a finer yarn. Allow for hem or fringe at both ends of rug.

If the rug is being made in sections, plan on a finished edge (page 29) at top and bottom of each section. Hemming flatweave sections is not advisable since a ridge will develop along joining lines. It is best to plan a flatweave that will incorporate the joinings as part of the design, as shown in photo on page 31. Allow for hems or fringes on those sections that will be at the top and bottom of the finished rug. Allow 3″ of warp for a finished edge, 2″ to 3″ for a hem, and 9″ for a fringe. *These are maximum lengths.* The allowance will be limited by the length of your loom.

Plain weave. This is the simplest construction in weaving and is the weave used in tapestries. It is like darning—the filling goes over every other end in one row, and under every other end in the next row. It forms the flatweave rugs and is the background for pile rugs. In one variation, a type of basket weave, the filling goes over two or three ends instead of one.

After a few picks, the shed sticks will probably be inadequate for beating down the filling, and you will have to use the beater for a more thorough job. The filling should be slack in the shed so that there will be enough to interweave comfortably around the warp ends. By inserting the filling at a diagonal, the yarn will have more slack and will cover the warp more completely. Begin the beating down at the selvedge where the filling entered and work across to where it exited. Further play for greater coverage can be obtained by bubbling (page 88)—a method of placing yarn in the shed in half circles. Press down on filling with finger or point of scissors to form curves. Hold filling loosely at point of exit and beat down.

The warp ends should always be maintained in a straight line. When you pull the filling around the selvedges, the warp may begin to narrow. A greater compression than ½″ to 1″ is undesirable since it is a condition that, once started, worsens with each pick. To prevent this happening, allow the yarn to lie somewhat loosely around the selvedges. Also, as the rug progresses, you can insert short lengths of warp yarns a couple of ends in from both selvedges of the rug body. Tie them tightly to the sides of the frame in order to keep the rug stretched to its intended width. Insert every inch or so, depending on how much the rug is being pulled in.

Note: If you want to try working without shed sticks, use a wooden needle to carry the filling and interweave it through the warp. The filling has to be the right thickness to pass through the eye of the needle. Use the beater to beat down filling.

Soumak. A flatweave rug is devoid of texture except where a textured yarn is used. A slightly textured surface can also be obtained

Two flatweave rugs. (Above left) Polish rug of wool on linen warp. (Above right) Greek rug of handspun, home-dyed wool on cotton warp. Woven by 15-year-old girl.

(Right) Rag rug on cotton warp. Rags are taffeta, velvet, corduroy, and cotton. Shuttle shown with rag strips wound around it.

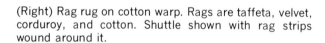

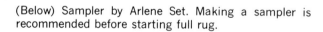

(Below) Sampler by Arlene Set. Making a sampler is recommended before starting full rug.

1½″ rya pile   cut flossa   4″ rya pile   soumak and plain weave   braid fringe

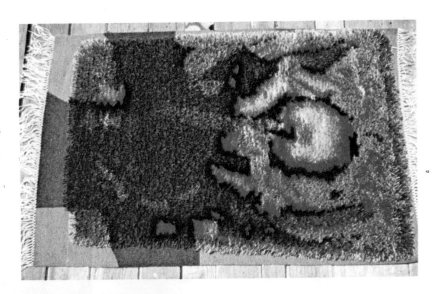

Rya rug by Anne Hornby. Border is
worked in flatweave.

Plain weave in a heavy yarn between
rows of cut and uncut flossa, by
Miriam Peck.

Free-form flatweave rug with knotted
pile, by Cynthia Schira. 38″ × 64″.

by use of the soumak technique, a v-shaped twining around the warp that gives a herringbone effect. It can be put in throughout the rug, or in rows, or in sections. The raised effect will be more pronounced with a heavier yarn. Since soumak is only meant to decorate the surface, a pick of plain weave is inserted after every one of soumak to give stability to the rug.

Do a pick of plain weave, from left to right, and close the shed. If you are using a new yarn for soumak, wind it in a butterfly or thread it through a bodkin, and secure it over and under the right selvedge. Do not pull yarn tight as you work or gaps will occur between the ends. A 4-2 soumak is shown, but any combination can be used. Just be sure that the resulting "floats" are not so long that someone could trip on them.

Knotted pile. Knotted pile is made with yarn formed into a butterfly. Since the background plain weave should not be visible, the yarn (or group of yarns) used must be thick enough to cover it. The amount of plain weave between rows depends on pile height: about 1″ between rows of 2″ pile, and ½″ between rows of 1″ pile. As rows are beaten down, the area compresses in width.

To make a flossa rug, use a pile gauge for an even pile (page 18). When beginning or ending a butterfly, leave its cut ends on the surface; then, if you wish, you can cut them below the level of the loops after the plain weave has been beaten down. For rya you can precut the yarn (page 18) or use your hand as the gauge for a random-length pile.

Since knots are usually not made on the selvedges, plain weave can be put in to maintain the strength of those edges. This can be done with filling yarn and shuttle or with a butterfly or bodkin in the same or in a heavier yarn. If desired, you can make the selvedge into a decorative edge by weaving a contrasting color yarn into it.

Finishing. Weave the top hem in the same manner as the bottom one. Since the edge filling picks may shift when the rug, or rug section, is taken off the loom, means must be provided for holding them in. Beginning at the bottom, start from the sevedges and work toward the center, cutting the ends pair by pair off the loom, a section at a time. Tie, in small, unobtrusive knots, according to the way the warp was made, 1 end by 1 end or 2 by 2, slipping the heading out as you go. Tie the knots tight and as close to the filling as possible. Do the same for the top of the rug, except there will be no heading to slip out. The knots are a momentary stopgap until you make a fringe (page 33) or add a finished edge (page 36). If you are not planning an edge such as a Swedish braid (page 29), double-knot the warp ends tightly, trim as close to the knot as possible, and turn back for a hem.

Sampler. Before you attempt a full-sized rug, try your hand at a sampler, incorporating whatever technique or techniques you wish. The sampler shown on page 91 consists of flatweave, soumak, different pile heights, and pile and flatweave combined.

TWO DESIGNS FOR WOVEN RUGS

Horizontal pattern

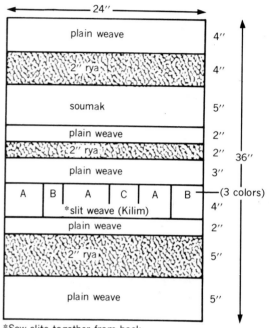

*Sew slits together from back

Counter balance pattern

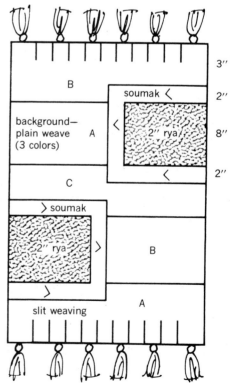

Suppliers

YARNS & GENERAL EQUIPMENT

Write for information regarding nearest distributor:

American Thread Co.
High Ridge Park
Stamford, Conn. 06905

Columbia-Minerva Corp.
295 5th Ave.
New York, N.Y. 10016

Emile Bernat & Sons Co.
P.O. Box 384
Uxbridge, Mass. 01569

Jack Frost Yarn Co.
207 Avenue C
New York, N.Y. 10009

Maysville Rug Yarns
January and Wood Co.
Maysville, Ky. 41056

Paternayan Bros., Inc.
312 E. 95th St.
New York, N.Y. 10028

Spinnerin Yarn Co., Inc.
230 5th Ave.
New York, N.Y. 10001

Susan Bates
C. J. Bates & Son, Inc.
Chester, Conn. 06412

TOOLS

Boye Needle Co., The
4335 No. Ravenswood Ave.
Chicago, Ill. 60613

J. L. Hammett Co. (frames)
Kendall Square
Cambridge, Mass. 02142

Scovill Manufacturing Co.
Oakville Div. (Dritz, Hero)
350 5th Ave.
New York, N.Y. 10001

Mail order suppliers for yarns and general equipment

Craft Yarns of Rhode Island, Inc.
603 Mineral Spring Avenue
Pawtucket, R.I. 02862

Dick Blick
P.O. Box 1267
Galesburg, Ill. 61401

Frederick Herrschner Co.
Hoover Rd.
Stevens Point, Wis. 54481

Kessenich Looms & Yarn Shop, Inc.
7463 Harwood Ave.
Wauwatosa, Wis. 53213

Lee Wards
P.O. Box 206
Elgin, Ill. 60120

Lily Mills Co.
Dept HWH
Shelby, N.C. 28150

Mannings, The
Creative Crafts School
R.D. 2
East Berlin, Pa. 17316

Needlecraft Shop, The
13561 Ventura Blvd.
Sherman Oaks, Calif. 91403

Niddy Noddy, The
1 Croton Point Avenue
Croton-on-Hudson, N.Y. 10520

School Products Co.
312 E. 23rd St.
New York, N.Y. 10010

Selma's Art Needlework
1645 2nd Ave.
New York, N.Y. 10028

Yarn Depot, Inc., The
545 Sutter St.
San Francisco, Calif. 94102

Scandinavian yarn and backing

"A Little Bit of Norway in Maryland"
Mrs. Bertha L. Knudsten
Parkton, Md. 21120

Coulter Studios, Inc.
138 E. 60th St.
New York, N.Y. 10022

CUM
Romersgade 5
Copenhagen, Denmark

House af Kleen
P.O. Box 224
No. Stonington, Conn. 06359

Dyes
(also hooking and braiding materials and equipment)

W. Cushing & Co.
"Perfection" Dyes
North St.
Kennebunkport, Me. 04046

Fabrics

Dorr Fabrics, Inc.
The Mill Store
Guild, N.H. 03754

Technique—Braiding

Gloria Walker Scannell
Wormer Road, R.D. #11
Voorheesville, N.Y. 12186

"Rags to Rugs"
Betty Pettibone
Route 37
New Fairfield, Conn. 06810

Technique—Hooking

George Wells
The Ruggery
Glen Head, N.Y. 11545

Norden Products
P.O. Box 1
Glenview, Ill. 60025

Rittermere Crafts Studio, Ltd.
P.O. Box 240
Vineland, Ontario, Canada

Schools and Workshops

The following is a partial list of schools and workshops that offer courses in Rugmaking. For further information write to the school direct.

Pendleton Fabric Craft School
Jordan Road, Box 233
Sedona, **Ariz.** 86336

Ida Grae Weaving and Design
424 La Verne
Mill Valley, **Calif.** 94941

The Yarn Depot, Inc.
545 Sutter St.
San Francisco, **Calif.** 94102

Brookfield Craft Center, Inc.
Brookfield, **Conn.** 06804

Associates Craft Workshops
Smithsonian Institution
Wash., D.C. 20560

Agnes Scott College
Decatur, **Ga.** 30030

Lincoln House
Old Sturbridge Village
Sturbridge, **Mass.** 01566

Workshops in Creative Arts
Boston YWCA
140 Clarendon St.
Boston, **Mass.** 02116

DeCordova Museum School of Art
Sandy Pond Road
Lincoln, **Mass.** 01773

Haystack School of Crafts
Deer Isle, **Me.** 04627

Plymouth Hoe Hand Craft Work Shop
Tenants Harbour, **Me.** 04860

Weiss Studio and Worship
161 Culberson Road
Basking Ridge, **N.J.** 07920

Denbrook House
(Stitch Witchery & The Cricket Cage)
Route 10, Box N
Denville, **N.J.** 07834

Brooklyn Museum Art School
Eastern P'kwy & Washington Ave.
Brooklyn, **N.Y.** 11238

Great Neck Public Schools
Adult Program
10 Arrandale Ave.
Great Neck, **N.Y.** 11024

The Niddy Noddy
1 Croton Pt. Ave.
Croton-on-Hudson, **N.Y.** 10520

Thousand Islands Museum Craft School
Clayton, **N.Y.** 13624

Penland School of Crafts
Penland, **N.C.** 28765

The Mannings
Creative Crafts School
R.D. 2
East Berlin, **Pa.** 17316

Richland Park YWCA
204 East Tyler
Richardson, **Tex.** 75080

Utah State Univ.
Dept. of Art
Logan, **Utah** 84321

The Factory of Visual Art
5040 9th Ave. N.E.
Seattle, **Wash.** 98105

Rittermere Crafts Studio, Ltd.
P.O. Box 240
Vineland, Ontario, **Canada**

For Further Reading

books

TECHNIQUES:

Allard, Mary, RUGMAKING: TECHNIQUES AND DESIGN, Chilton Co., Philadelphia, Pa., 1963

Beitler, Ethel J., CREATE WITH YARN, International Textbook Co., Scranton, Pa., 1964

Brinley, Rosemary, RUGMAKING, Distributed by Wehman Bros., Hackensack, N.J., 1955

Collingwood, Peter, THE TECHNIQUES OF RUG WEAVING, Watson-Guptill Publications, New York, N.Y., 1969

De Dillmont, Therese, ENCYCLOPEDIA OF NEEDLEWORK (D.M.C. Library) eds. Th. D. Dillmont, Mulhouse, Alsace, France (no date)

Feeley, Helen H., THE COMPLETE BOOK OF RUG BRAIDING, Coward-McCann, Inc., New York, N.Y., 1963

Green, Sylvia, CANVAS EMBROIDERY FOR BEGINNERS, Watson-Guptill Publications, New York, N.Y., 1970

Kirsch, Dietrich, and Kirsch-Korn, Jutta, MAKE YOUR OWN RUGS, Watson-Guptill Publications, New York, N.Y., 1969

Lawless, Dorothy, RUG HOOKING AND BRAIDING FOR PLEASURE AND PROFIT, T. Y. Crowell Co., New York, N.Y., 1962

Phillips, Mary Walker, STEP-BY-STEP KNITTING, Golden Press, New York, N.Y., 1967

Putnam, Dorothy P., BEAUTIFUL BRAIDING, Asa Bartlett Press, Worcester, Mass., 1960

Thomas, Mary, MARY THOMAS'S DICTIONARY OF EMBROIDERY STITCHES, Gramercy Publishing Co., New York, N.Y., 1935

Wiseman, Ann. RAG TAPESTRIES AND WOOL MOSAICS, Van Nostrand-Reinhold Co., New York, N.Y., 1969

Znamierowski, Nell, STEP-BY-STEP WEAVING, Golden Press, New York, N.Y., 1967

GENERAL:

Adrosko, Rita J., NATURAL DYES AND HOME DYEING, Dover Publications, Inc., New York, N.Y., 1971

Brooklyn Botanical Garden, DYE PLANTS AND DYEING—A HANDBOOK, Brooklyn, N.Y., 1964

Chevreul, M. E., THE PRINCIPLES OF HARMONY AND CONTRAST OF COLORS AND THEIR APPLICATION TO THE ARTS, Van Nostrand-Reinhold Co., New York, N.Y., 1967

Conley, Emma, VEGETABLE DYEING, Penland School of Handicrafts Inc., Penland, N.C.

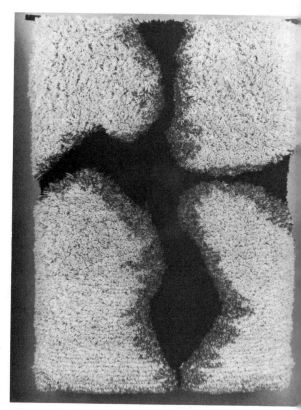

"Fjord," by Park Chambers, Jr. 45" × 65". Black, gray, and white rya woven of wool on linen warp. Photo by Richard Margolis.

"Exit, Bye, Bye," designed and woven by Carol Lubove.

Garrett, Lillian, VISUAL DESIGN: A PROBLEM SOLVING AP-PROACH, Van Nostrand-Reinhold Co., New York, N.Y., 1967

Itten, Johannes, THE ELEMENTS OF COLOR, Van Nostrand-Reinhold Co., New York, N.Y., 1970

Roth, Rodris, FLOOR COVERINGS IN 18th-CENTURY AMERI-CA, Smithsonian Press, Washington, D.C., 1967

Smith, Charles N., STUDENT HANDBOOK OF COLOR, Van Nostrand-Reinhold Co., New York, N.Y., 1965

periodicals

Craft Horizons, The American Craftsmen's Council, 16 E. 52nd St., New York, N.Y. 10022

Handweaver & Craftsman, 220 5th Ave., New York, N.Y. 10001

Needle Arts, The Embroiderers' Guild of America, Inc., 120 E. 56th St., New York, N.Y. 10022

Shuttle Spindle & Dye Pot, Handweavers' Guild of America, 339 N. Steele Rd., West Hartford, Conn. 06117

Book Services

Craft & Hobby Book Service, P.O. Box 626, Pacific Grove, Calif. 93950

Museum Books, Inc., 48 E. 43rd St., New York, N.Y. 10017

The Unicorn, Box 645-F, Rockville, Md. 20851